C000161665

A Guide to Surviving Childhood
Look, Mum, You Sh*t Yourself

By Maxie Reynolds

A Guide to Surviving Childhood is a work of non-fiction. Nonetheless, some names and personal characteristics of individuals or events have been changed in order to disguise identities. Any resulting resemblance to persons living or dead is entirely coincidental and unintentional.

Maxie Reynolds Publishing. Paperback First Edition
Copyright © 2019 by Maxie Reynolds
All rights reserved. No part of this publication may be reproduced or transmitted in any form or by any means, electronic or mechanical, including photocopies or recording, or any information storage and retrieval system known or to be invented, without permission in writing from the publisher, except by a reviewer who wishes to quote brief passages in connection with a review written for inclusion in a magazine, newspaper or broadcast.

Printed in Scotland. For information, write to In Doggo Publishing, 407 Lincoln Road, Miami Beach, FL, 33139.

www.maxiereynolds.com

UK Copyright: A Guide to Surviving Childhood: Look Mum You Shit Yourself

All photos courtesy of the author unless otherwise indicated.
Library of Congress Cataloguing-in-publication Data is available from the Library of Congress.

ISBN: 978-1-9161519-4-9

This book may be purchased in bulk for promotional, educational or business use. Please contact your local bookseller or Maxie Reynolds Ltd via email at book@maxiereynolds.com

First Edition: November 2019
Cover by Maxie Reynolds

FOR MY MUM AND ODDS, WHO'VE TAUGHT ME THE
MOST, BUT WHO STILL AREN'T GETTING ANY OF THE
PROCEEDS FROM THIS BOOK.
TO BOTH OF YOU: ~~THANK~~ FIGHT ME.

Prefacey McPreface

It's semi-important, if you care about notes, to note the following notes:

1. It's called *A Guide to Surviving Childhood* but is not a child-friendly book.

2. It contains a lot of swearing. Olympic Gold levels of just unneeded fucking cursing and other such fuckery. No refunds, friends. No refunds.

3. Shake off all the heinous names I call my mum in this book. She likes them, honestly. In fact, she loves them. She usually asks me to call her more names. She cries tears of laughter at them all the time (no, you're lying on the first page!).

4. The overall tone and fashion in which conversations between myself and my mum are relayed aren't to be taken *that* seriously. I mean, if child services didn't take them seriously, why would you? (*Laughs nervously.)

As kids, we take things differently than adults intend – that's the business of being a kid. And it makes looking back and telling stories all the more fun (in most cases). Plus, it'd be really, really awful to go through your childhood with the mind of an adult.

5. By the time I was 15, we'd lived in nearly twenty houses in and around Dundee. It would make reading this book like reading the BT Phone Book if I listed them all, so I mainly just give out areas and sh*t jokes to go along with them. (Oh, stop it! I know, I write so well it's a miracle this is my first book.)

6. There is not an age that exists at which you can tell your mum that your friend has been an arsehole – that's just a general note that shouldn't be ignored. There's. No. Going. Back.

7. Don't let this book put you off going to visit Dundee in Scotland. It's an amazing little place!

The Bit with All the Chapter Titles

It fell off the back of a lorry (truck)

I'm going to see a man about a dog! (And he was always 'sold out')

That time I ran away and the police brought me home

I'm not scared to put you on your arse in front of anyone, dear!

I'm not scared to put you on your arse in front of anyone, dear! (in front of a police officer)

Another 'amusing' example

Be! *Be*cause!

I'm not here to be your friend!

Oh fucking really!

I'm the adult and you're the child

If your friends jumped off the bridge, would you?

Because I'm the adult and you're the child – part two

Don't you dare

I am not a monster – Myra Hindley is a monster! Do you want me to go and get her?

Call me 'Auntie Max' when we get in here

You'll be pretty when you grow up and you're beautiful to me!

I know you're lying to me!

Drinking is bad for you

No … Because I said so, that's why! (Sometimes said as 'Can you buggery!')

No! That's not right!

I'll make you one – the one with the Provy man

Can I borrow your pocket money?

You know I will never love another person on this planet as much as I love you!

Part Two: You Can Always Talk to Me About …

Boys

Drugs

Sex

School

Part Three: Things Iraq Torture Techniques Couldn't Get Me to Say to My Mum Ever Again

1. I've lost (insert any item of clothing, including socks, here)

2. I wasn't at school

3. It's peaceful to drown

4. I didn't take the dog to the pound

5. You didn't take the dog to an adoption farm

6. Can I stay out later? … The bus was late

7. Can you stop smoking so I can have dinner money?

8. You're embarrassing me!

9. Your butt jiggles like jelly

10. You don't suit that fringe!

11. I know who my dad is …

12. I've been swapping the painkillers out with your medicine

13. I don't know how all my presents got tears in the paper!

14. It's ridiculous. Just get a black carpet!

Part Four: My Mum on the Importance of …

Tea/dinnertime

Being in a routine

Not smoking

Exercise

Surgery

Not dressing like a lesbian

Part Five: What My Mum Did When I …

Asked her if she was sure someone would want to marry me when I was older

Forgot my key

Said flies might be sending me messages

Told her I'd thought about pushing her out of the kitchen window

Told her I'd said to my friend's mum that she'd told me said mum was a lesbian

Got her clothes pegs for Christmas

Told her girls were mean to me

Tried smoking

Took advantage of a two-for-one offer

Cut myself bangs

Ran away from her and then locked her out

Asked her if the lights went off when I blinked

Took too long to pick sweets

Nearly re-entered the room after my bird died

Told her my aunt and uncle used me as a drug mule

Failed to be grateful enough

Part Six: Things She's Made Up

That she'd bought me a car

Butter on my slippers

Your dad is …
i. dead
ii. in the military
iii. dead to us

My sister

Her middle name

That I just turned my pants inside out

My (insert family member here) died (I'll always keep you alive)

Things I did that might have made her this way

The end

How she wants you to think it was.

How it really was...

The Start: A Little About Her and a Little About Us

This is a collection of stories from my mum's childhood as she raised me through mine. She's Big Max, our family overlord, and I'm Wee Max, the family know-it-all. It can't be helped. People have prayed to the baby Lord Jesus. Men have wept.

Friends have tried to saw me off. But alas, I'm close to insufferable and I keep it going for fun.

Fight me thrice.

I'm 5′8″ and she's 5′3″ but she's got a big mouth and a bigger temper, so we call her Big Max. To her face, we tell her it's cute and we like that she's *passionate*. Behind her back, we say that she's a c*nt. I'M KIDDING! GOD!

We say she's a massive c*nt.

Big Max had me when she was 17 years old in Dundee, Scotland. Her mother was an alcoholic at the time; her father was starting a whole new life with another woman, who used to be a secret but wasn't a secret anymore; her eldest brother had just died after sniffing glue; and my now estranged father was out robbing old, abandoned factories around the city of Dundee, which is how we came to have a hospital bed as both 'day bed' (aka a sofa) and night bed (aka a bed).

Big Max herself had just left ~~boarding school~~ the care system, and her readjustment back into society was ... interesting. We are, and always have been, a busy family.

Globally, though, '88 was a good year: laws restricting opening times for UK pubs changed, and so the bulk of the Scottish population could stay out all day to get ready for all night; the Soviet Red Army withdrew from Afghanistan and cleared a space for Bush; and I was born in a surprise slip-and-slide entrance three months too early for anyone's liking.

By coming out a bit early, I looked a lot like a baby scrotum. If you imagine a small face pressed into a really big sack of old ball skin, that's how I looked, but with jaundice, too. Anyway, thanks to my early debut, the nursery room, Mothercare wardrobe, along with my 400-detachable-parts pram and an appropriate store of Huggies terry towelling nappies, were nowhere in sight. We had to settle for a flat in Ardler, Dundee, with one carpeted room, living off the emergency credit and trading our milk tokens for cigarettes and chocolate from a shop off of McAlpine Road. Wasn't all that bad, actually. We enjoyed it.

Although it might have been in our best financial interests to be adopted. Or die.

When I first got out of the joint, we had a good run. A solid two-and-a-half years were had by all. I ate and giggled a lot. She got to dress me up in adorable little outfits that I'd spew on. What's not to love? The teamwork was second to none!

We went far and wide and up and down (the multis) together and people gave us things for free, like attention and food – all because I existed. She was my best friend and first love.

Then, in the blink of my cockeye, she absolutely hated me, and I was beginning to become less fond of her.

We started eating with different family members at different times, and she started to sleep longer in the mornings, while I drew on the walls and overdosed on my gran's medications – a fun story for later.

I'm hoping, even though I said it like a heartless b*stard, that that last bit is relatable (minus the meds). Motherhood is hard. You can tell it's hard from being the kid of someone who finds it hard, and when you get older, you can either have your own and find out it's hard, or you can ask a close friend – both of which will probably result in you finding out parenthood is ... (start the drumroll) hard.

Thanks for coming to my TED Talk. Hope you all feel better now.

Kidding. You've got a few more pages to get through, alas.

From those moving topics to this: is it fascinating to anyone else how to a child everyone a lot older or even just a lot taller is definitely an adult. You see them as twice the size and one thousand times more capable than they are. It's automatically assumed they are a person who has infinite wisdom, can solve any problem, knows what to say at any given moment and can be trusted with complex tasks, like making food *and* telling you the time?

They have answers to questions you haven't even thought of yet and everything they do is adult-cool. Sometimes, though, in reality, they are just teenagers that got pupped up too early.

And so say hello to Big Max.

She pedal-to-the-metaled parenthood, putting just about everything she had into not raising a moron. She did okay on that latter goal. Not great, but okay. And there's still time for me to turbo-ruin this, so we won't know for sure for another 50–60 years.

The differences

If you're 50 years old or younger, there's a good chance you can clearly identify the same generational disparities as me: our parents had their shit somewhat more together than us. I don't know who to blame for this widening aperture, but like everything else these days, it's Trump or social media.

Let's compare and take a small, fondly coloured look at some of the differences between my mum and me. We'll start with me at 18 and then her: I was living life to the fullest. Taking every opportunity that came my way and making waves.

Sorry, that whole last sentence was a typo. I was frequenting Fatty's (a nightclub in the centre of Dundee) three times per week and returning outfits to Primark on a Monday morning, floating around on this rock with no real discernible goals or ambition and trying to convince suspected OAPs that techno was the new rock 'n' roll.

It was not. DJ Rankin was a poor choice of idol. I regret it all.

For all its faults, such as overpriced alcohol and open drug deals, Fatty's, once Dundee's pre-eminent nightclub, actually taught me a lot about life – things that Big Max just couldn't.

All things taught:
- Nothing good happens after 2 a.m.
- The ladies' toilets can and will be used as a boxing ring.
- I will pimp any of my mates out to a bouncer to avoid paying the ten quid entry fee.
- Legally being classed as an adult does not make you an adult. It makes you a really funny liability to observe.

Fatty's was also where I had a lot of my starter-scrapes with the lowest of the low. One guy in a wheelchair, for example, really took a loan me.

How that happened

The other problem with Fatty's was that they used to pack us in there. There were reports of STIs being passed by proxy. I myself nearly accidentally got finger-banged in there thrice – and that's just remembering the cases in which men were trying to retrieve their wallets from their trousers … or check it was still there. Fatty's also had a problem with pickpockets.

One night, I escaped up to the third floor where it was mainly old dears dancing around their handbags, just giving it all their hips could take to any song by Journey. But what also happened on this floor was that people in wheelchairs would congregate. It was like *Cars* for adults, but a lot better.

We used to place bets and watch them race one another. Not in a sick way, obvs. The winner also used to enjoy the victory lap and we'd all low-five them on their way round.

Is it insensitive, though? Is it really?

Long story short, one chair dweller sweetly agreed to give me a lift home if I ~~necked with~~ kissed him. So, inevitably, I summoned all the dignity and self-respect I had, and, in no uncertain terms, I told him that I absolutely would. And then I did. Shocking, I know. You just don't think a man in a wheelchair would take advantage of an able-bodied teen, but here I am – the proof that it happens.

So, having got lucky, as in he had an electric wheelchair, off we went. I didn't live that far away and, as fate would have it, neither did he. Glad not to be taking him too far out of his way, I felt good about it all ('it all' mainly being his battery life and his technically drunk driving).

I slung my heels in his back basket and sat on his lap. He didn't have to adjust a thing to compensate for my weight, because he couldn't feel anything from the waist down.

He strapped me in, and, with my hair blowing in the wind, I became unsure if saying, 'Onwards, noble steed' would be better or worse than, 'I'm flying, Jack, I'm flying!' But the chances of his actual name being Jack were slim, so I opted for the former. A nicety I shouldn't have afforded him, because that d*ckbag, not ten minutes later, tried to finger-bang me under a flickering streetlamp. And his wallet and phone were in his side carry, so it was no mistake!

With his left hand on forward, he tried to slip his right hand up my skirt. I was raging. I said, 'If you think I'm going to sit here and subject myself to this ... you'd be right, because I cannot seem to undo this seatbelt!'

Could I even remotely get to the seatbelt buckle? NO. I could not. His leg was like a deadweight, and I couldn't lift it from my position on his lap, as hard as I tried. As we got to the top of Strathmartine Road, the guy from the kebab shop came out and started screaming in my defence.

'You can't do that!' he blasted. 'That's sick! That's meant for people who need it!'

I was thinking, *That's an odd way to put it, but, yeah, Glitzy (don't lie, we all name our private parts) is not meant to be attacked by four-wheeled foes in the night! She might be needed in a close-to-pristine state by Brad Pitt in the near future.*

Did you hear that? That was the sound of the tone being lowered. Took me longer than initially expected. I'm feeling pretty good about it though.

I say all of this because I really did think I was an adult. There was no indication I wasn't; Big Max wasn't really telling me what to do anymore. No one else was telling me what to do. I was allowed where there were other adults.

I was, of course, looking for a boyfriend on these nights out, because grown-ups also have boyfriends, right? Like a lot of teens, I hadn't yet concluded that relationships are 70% nightmare, 20% fun and 10% comparison to other, also shit, relationships.

I hadn't even worked out that all adulthood means is that you don't have to ask for money, you have to make it; all of your mates do cocaine with their apprentice pay packets; and you make your own doctor's appointments or die.

Let's all stop having kids, and then when the last generation has grown up, we'll all revert to how life was when we under ten years old. It'll be great, because sooner or later, everyone seems to come to the same realisation: that what we thought being an adult was going to be like is nothing, nada, zilch, zero, diddly-squat like the reality.

We all wanted to be adults, and just take a fucking look at us. **LOOK AT US!**

All this was to say, I think I expected more of my mum just because she was a mum.

Now for Big Max at 18: she had me and an Argos catalogue scrapbook dream she was determined never to let die. She was not taking lifts from Warm Wheels in the night.

She was tugging the responsibility of a human life around with her. A little human who just never stopped, never slept, never just *shhhhhh'd*. *And* who thought her mum's only purpose on Earth was to be just that: a mum. She was to do mum things and to act mum-like at all times.

Being a parent looks like it's giving up a lot of yourself for not *that* much in return. I reckon it's mainly because there's no way for any of us to tell that you weren't born to be our parents.

Life is cruel. Can I get a ~~'Amen'~~ 'Kids are sh*t sometimes'?

Like most mums, Big Max always tried hard and, even now, when she could be on an over-40s cruise in Ibiza trying to get herself a toy boy and millennial clap, she calls me once a week to make sure I still need her, tells me if there's been a rape or murder within a 400-mile radius of where I am, laughs at all my jokes and hates the same people I do. She always takes my side and she loves me the way only a mother can. (No, you shut up. You're getting emotional before the first chapter!)

It's just a shame that we don't know to appreciate our parents until we're older and far, *far* more jaded.

When I told her I was writing a book that I hoped would one day hold many cups of coffee on it in houses all throughout the land, she said to me, 'I think that's a wonderful idea, Max. Everyone has a mum, and some of them might even be able to see a bit of their own in me ... Unless you write it like I was a lunatic.'

I tried to keep the book factual on all levels, so obviously she was going to come across as a lunatic. The bi*ch is CRAZY. But she didn't drink wine, so she had to do it all within the dark confines of sobriety. There are Mondays I can't get through without wine. Well done, Big Max. Well done mums – wine or no wine.

All in all, this is the story of one woman's struggle and, according to the people who matter most, triumph against the odds of bringing a child up alone from too young an age.

Big Max was a boss. I just didn't know it. I reckon it's that way for a lot of kids looking at their parents. So: Dear parents, we are sorry. If we aren't now, we will be when we have our own children.

Finally, I've purposely kept the first few stories short and semi-sweet, half to trick you into thinking this book is going to be far more pleasant than it is, and half to not make us all suicidal in the first chapter. In any case, they should serve as a good introduction to Big Max – my mum, my dad and my best friend.

Most of us have the same favourite childhood memories: looking forward to the mail for some reason and not understanding bills. And thinking our pets understood us and were waiting for the right time to talk back.

Part One: Things Said in Our House

The top 11 most-said things in our house

1. Be there in a minute ...

As a three-year-old, there are many things you can do: you can sing, dance and do dumb, dumb, really dumb things without anyone thinking you're mentally challenged.

You can get the tightest bastards in the world to give you small amounts of cash for no good reason, and you can even take a poop in peace, but you cannot wipe without your back needing to be bleached and all the toilet roll being being used. Big Max was readily aware of this handicap.

I was an independent child, I think; I used to go to the bathroom with paper (A4) and crayons, and, at the same time as being proud I'd made it clean through the day, I would try not to fall down the toilet.

We all know the stance; don't make me describe it. Okay, I'll do it: butt not hitting either side of the seat, two arms poker straight on either side, butthole like a rabbit's.

My mum, while waiting on me finishing my daily task, would presumably be doing adult things in the living room, like hoping I was backed up or plotting ways to make me too tired to talk. Children do talk too much, so no one blames her.

But once, knowing of and counting on the inability to tear, fold, bend and wipe, she left three-year-old me on the toilet for an hour and a half while she watched soaps with my three aunts, all the while hearing me shout, 'Mum! Mummmmmy! I've finished pooping now, Mum! I just need you to wipe my bum now, Mummy ... *Mummmmmmy?*'

Nothing.

Guiding tip: Dump when an adult is taking a bath.

There's a good chance I peaked in '91 though. The fact I'm legally an adult today is hilarious.

2. Go ahead, make my day!

From about one foot tall and onwards, all I heard was, 'Go ahead, make my day!'

I don't know about you fine folk, but for me, there's no possible way to list the times I heard spine-curling phrases like this gem.

But I can tell you that they were often followed up with, 'Shut up, or I'll give you something to cry about!' And that gave me the feeling that all the Disney princesses on my pants were about to look like some really tanned bitches. Jasmine would obviously look black.

Big Max used to run entirely on nicotine and anger, but if you annoyed her before the nicotine part, you were assured verbal, if not physical, annihilation.

One day she walked me to school, not because she was actually walking me to school but because she was out of cigarettes and my school was near the shop.

On the way, I fell over a really huge, massive, enormous pebble, and she turned into Kim Jong-un.

All I said back was, 'It's not my fault that stone tripped me' – but before I could finish, her famous grimace had taken over her face and her teeth were poking out like tiny sharp knives.

She growled, 'Go ahead, make my day!', in a voice that sounded like it was dragging itself out of her. Then she picked me up off the ground and hauled me all the way to the school gate by my writing arm, all the while telling me I would make her day if I uttered a single sound.

But what didn't help was that on my way back from school, I accidentally peed a little while wearing white tights and, in a moment of pure genius, tried to blame it on tripping over the same stone again.

Guiding tip: Adults are rarely friendly in the mornings. Avoid at all costs. Don't mention anything you've tried to blame before.

Note: while the first two stories would tend to prove otherwise, I didn't actually ever have a problem with my bladder or poop chute … Sort of.

3. No, you can't dress yourself … because people will think I dressed you!

This from the woman who once made me go ice skating in a skirt. I tried to reason with her, but alas she sent me onto a frozen pool of water with knee-length pink frills as protection.

It was not ideal.

I nearly went Tonya Harding on her twice. Firstly, I could've for sure been a pro skater, but probably more of the hockey variety and likely the goalkeeper. And two, I could've definitely hired someone to take my mum down a peg or two.

By the end of that day, and what was essentially the end of my skating career, I looked like I had cerebral palsy, but I felt a lot more sorry for myself than the people I know with actual cerebral palsy. It took me three consecutive baths to persuade my gran to shout at Big Max to make me feel warm again.

So, back to the point in hand – I was under no circumstances allowed to dress myself. There was an exception to the rule, though: every single day I was allowed to dress myself, but only for school. Not out of the will to let me grow and evolve as a child, but because she hated mornings and we had a uniform.

How I ended her morning slumbers

Unfortunately, she had to forgo her usual morning-through-to-afternoon snooze after St. Fergus Primary School called her to let her know they would be sending me home a few hours early that day because I had shown up wearing thongs.

Our headmistress did not see the ingenuity nor appreciate the time it'd taken me to understand how they should be worn (yeah, obviously I had them on backwards) or the nimbleness it'd taken to tie a knot on either side just so they'd stay up. The real show-stopping moment was when my mates and I put pencils through the holes to see if I could draw a circle with a full turn between two desks. It was likely the giveaway, too.

When I got home, my mum explained to me that her pants were different from mine and not just in size, but also in style and function. Not one to carry stories, I thought I should keep to myself the fact that Mrs Rudy had also said the devil wore thongs and that they were unnatural.

But I didn't keep it to myself. I told her.

Then, in a fleeting moment of pure innocence and sheer good-heartedness, I offered to get some pants off of my gran for her.

She declined the offer.

Guiding tip: Do you know how long it takes kids to get dressed? AGES! You could be downstairs taking Valium and Xanax and loving life in the time it takes a small child to get ready. First, hide their favourite things in places that will slow them, and when they finally come down looking like a Teletubby that got violently kicked through the Disney Store, tell them that they need to go back up and find their armbands and swim-ring because there's a chance it'll rain. Then nap.

Guiding tip 2: Read the previous paragraph and note it down somewhere. Send a thank you email to me.

4. I've got eyes in the back of my head!

Obviously, this was a straight-out and straight-up lie and she played me like a second-hand fiddle.

Getting past the confusion this causes children who are visual learners, there was a time when I was about two feet tall and obsessed with learning to fly. I'd ended up on the outside of our window ledge, looking down at the ground about

15 storeys below. She'd always said she'd know if I was doing anything naughty because one set of her eyes would always be watching me.

Well, not that day! She was living in the hope that the Allfather was keeping an eye on me.

'I've got eyes in the back of my head' died out not too long after that almost-fatal incident.

There does come a point in all of our lives when we realise our parents are a-holes and they spend a large amount of their time lying to us. This is what first led me to that sad, sad understanding, and, more importantly, it was the catalyst that let me realise my own potential as a colourful and convincing ~~liar~~ embellisher.

Guiding tip: What doesn't kill you makes you ~~stro~~ prone to other moronic actions.

5. You little basket case, get over here now!

Yeah, wait and I'll just take a run straight into your loving arms ...

No, thank you.

Again, not one of my favourites. It's also not the call to action I'd use as a parent.

Guiding tip: Remember this, then trick your own children with a soft voice so they come to you, and then you can beat them like a drum.

We've come to the midway point of the first chapter, and I just wanted to say (1) thanks for reading, (2) still no refunds and (3) if any of these have made you think about your own childhood and inspired a book, I'm on 10%. And also, (4) how much do you wish you'd just bought a novel?

6. Go to the shops

I had to walk to the shops so often that Unicef were thinking about sponsoring me.

If Adidas knew about Dundee, I'd have had 2012 Yeezys in 2002. (Probably not the worst joke in this book. Don't shut it, though. Don't give up. You're better than that. Stay with me.)

Like most children, I underwent ~~six hours of schooling~~ one hour of schooling, plus five hours of giving teachers uncalled-for and uninvited abuse five days out of seven. And like most children, I was still a slave afterwards, but that's how you've got to roll if you want to skim the change from the milk.

However, if 'Go to the shops' was uttered in our household before the 8.05 a.m. mark, which happened to be the exact time I left to catch the bus for school, then I knew I was f*cked.

For one, adults are more on the ball in the mornings and will notice if you halve their change, so I generally tried to avoid that situation by brushing my teeth out of my bedroom window and chugging my dry Weetabix before her first kettle of the day had boiled.

One day, though, the 'request' came in at about 4 p.m. – the time I got home each day from being bullied by my mates and being an arsehole to fellow students who weren't my mates.

I found my mum in her usual sedentary position, with one difference: this particular day, she was holding an ashtray under her chin with one hand, and a needle poked through a lit cigarette butt in the other. In Dundee, we call that 'smoking the beef'. It was like looking at moving poetry.

The fragile-looking mother of one said softly, but softly like a smoker does, 'Please, Max,' and tilted her head down to look again at the theatre of atrocities happening just under her chin, 'go to the shops for your old mum!' She then flashed a half-crooked smile, which I think was meant to soften me, and it did ... given I would be able to tell the Naz all about it.

Naz, my local sugar dealer, was actually one of my best childhood friends, even though he must have been about 50 years old at the time and hated kids.

He was like Apu from *The Simpsons*, or maybe more of a Naveed from *Still Game*, but without the accent and slightly more willing to break the law, which both Big Max and I remain level 478398909 thankful for – just if we had to put a rough number on it. He sold me cigarettes for her because (1) he was scared of her, and (2) I was adorable.

We'd become friends, Naz and I, because I frequented his shop a lot and needed him to like me because one day I hoped he'd sell me alcohol knowing I was an underager. As I was walking triumphantly towards his place, I thought to myself that nothing could beat the picture I was going to paint of the 30-something-year-old woman sitting in a dark living room with no cigarettes, no self-respect, no dignity, no hope, no friends, no self-will, no control, no discipline and no restraint, and smoking butt ends with a needle out of sheer desperation tightly bound to utter laziness.

And I was right.

He even gave me a box of Dairylea Dunkers that were about to go out of date and a handful of Marble bars that had been melted by the sun as a show of his gratitude.

There was also no way Kev the Alchy, as he was affectionately known by me, was going to have a better story when he came in from Harlequins next door.

When I got back to the house with her 20 fags and can of Coke, she retired the needle and smiled softly. They were some of the best minutes of our young life together.

I just took a DNA test, turns out I'm 100% that snitch...

(Brought to you in part by Lizzo and in part by my being a snitch.)

7. You can be anything you want to be ... not that!

Big Max always, always, always x 10,000,000 said that I could be absolutely anything I wanted to be. That's why I tend to do sweet eff all day-to-day now. Kidding. I do loads. It's just not that productive or helpful to mankind.

She used to tell me all the time, and still reminds me to this day, that it doesn't matter where you're from, what you started out with or who you know or don't know, you can be and do whatever you want – hence why in the St. Fergus Primary School yearbook I expressly stated my wish to be nothing less than an astronaut.

I'm Dundee's Hodor. That. Was. Never. Going. To. Happen. But we believed.

She told me time and time again that whatever I wanted to be was, with some hard work and perseverance, well within my reach.

Until I wanted to be a singer.

Don't get me wrong, I was still working towards becoming an astronaut, but it was a grind: we weren't able to afford the Kellogg's mini variety packs during the period they were putting planetary information on the back of them, and I was deep in my own personal Dark Age – a time before I'd heard of Neil deGrasse Tyson.

Nine-year-old me was pretty humped.

So, I had to temporarily relinquish my dream of being the first girl named Max in space and settle for the bright lights of the stage instead.

I felt I was about to become a pop sensation from the age of nine (to around the age of ~~30~~ 15).

I wanted to sing a mishmash of Celine Dion- and Eminem-themed songs on festival stages the world over, marry Gareth Gates, kill Jordan for sleeping with my future man and defiling him, and then have cute, possibly stuttering, babies.

I mispredicted the future. You cannot have everything you want in this life.

My mum refused to take me to an audition in Glasgow even though she was the one who told me about an audition in Glasgow ... It would probably have been my one big missed shot at stardom, but someone made the grave error of actually taking me. I was about to find out that I sounded like, as the great legend that is Deadpool once said, 'a wheezing bag of dick tips'.

Let me set the scene: I'd been singing loudly in and around the house for weeks, and she'd asked if I was still sure I wanted to be a pop star. I replied that I obviously did and asked if she really thought I was going to let the lyrical genius in me go to waste.

I remember her reply in all its glory, down to its verbal speed. She said, 'Well, if that's really what you want to be, then I think, maybe, you need to take some singing lessons.'

To which I logically replied, 'Okay, so will you find some for me?'

Her answer: 'No.'

Not one to let a vicious act of sabotage stifle me, I got my uncle Mike to take me to the audition for the girl band in Glasgow that was to release my inner Adele.

Enter: the wheezing bag of dick tips.

When it came to my turn to sing, my saliva turned to powder and my voice came out like I was maybe dying at that very moment. My face turned race-car red and I felt a lot like I'd sh*t myself.

The judges were pretty nice, though. Not only did they not laugh before I'd *nearly* left the room, but one of them also said, 'Don't give up!', and I think another also said, mid laugh – nay, mid flu cough, in July – 'See [receptionist] on your way out for the names of recommended singing coaches.'

I already knew that singing lessons were a no-go and so that dream died a croaky death. But a new dream developed: I wanted to be a policewoman.

This was also gently ripped from me.

Big Max didn't come right out and say that the reason she didn't want me to join Dundee's Finest was because she was pretty well known to them; instead, she went with the always persuasive appeal – or lack of, in this case – of money.

She told me the police didn't get paid enough for what they had to do and put up with, and I confirmed this was true when I asked the policeman on guard just outside our house on Princes Street in Dundee.

He was stood in the pissing rain for a 12-hour shift in front of a door to a building where there had been a suspicious fire blazing a day or two before. A few people, including a baby, had been forced to jump out of their window, two storeys up, onto the presumably less heated tarmac below.

I said to him, 'I want to join the police, but my mum said you don't get paid enough for what you do', and then I waited for confirmation while making direct eye contact with him the entire time, like any normal creepy kid.

He looked down at me, moved his hat upwards and said, 'Not only that, lass, but these boots cannae outrun a pair of stolen Reeboks anymore.'

I looked at him with my eyebrows furrowed, trying to express the feeling of sorrow I felt for him, and said, 'I think they (the Reebok-wearing criminals) usually hide behind something until you leave the neighbourhood. Maybe you can trick them in future!'

That's right: I was a snitch before I even knew what a snitch was.

He gave me a little pat on the back and told me that there was a good chance I'd make the force, but that I should join somewhere like the

Orkney Islands or Dorset where the crime rate is minus zero.

Alas, not too long after that, relatively speaking, my door was kicked in by a couple of pairs of those boots, even though it had a letterbox they could've just tapped lightly in order to get my attention.

I was 'questioned' or, more accurately put, badgered about and accused of a crime I didn't commit, even though my innocence was steadfastly apparent.

The 'bad cop' that day told me that they had video evidence of me stealing my friend's mum's car. Knowing that I was innocent, for once, I asked to see this magical proof, and they were forced to scoot.

None of the other clichés applied that day. No other movie moments were had. They didn't ask me to come down to the station for further questioning, and they offered me nothing to talk about the guy next door with a meth lab, which I couldn't have talked about even if I wanted to. Baz used to bring me baked goods in the morning because he never ever slept. Simple *meth* really – why would I ever want Baz locked up?

They were also in my living room, which I've never seen in a movie.

After a few more run-ins with the police, I understood some of the reasons why people had Reeboks to outrun them.

My friend and I did try shoplifting once and I did get caught when my nerve rash made its pretty inopportune appearance as I tried to exit with about 30 pieces of clothing.

Obviously, I told them the truth straight away: I'd forgotten to pay for all of them, and, yeah, I was sure I hadn't brought my own Asda bag to the city centre.

I got put in a cell with a heroin addict and we had a pretty informative little heart to heart. She let me ask her questions and gave me some reliable facts, such as the reason most addicts look like they don't bathe is because they don't bathe.

The water feels like little needles on their skin and they'd rather be shooting up.

Seems fair.

She also said the police framed her and she had no idea how the frozen roast chicken from Marks & Spencer got up her jumper. I believed her.

Good time to note that I'm not ashamed of myself – that's my mum's job.

Plus, it was one time and I was about 16 years old. Let's not get too high and mighty, because those who live in glass houses better have really good insurance.

What's funny about it is that when I came to live in America, I spent the first few months getting really annoyed at the staff in clothes shops for following me around. There's no way the Tayside police's reach went that far. Right?

Yeah, it's pretty bob-on. They are just really helpful in Beverly Hills. Same job as the staff in Dundee's shops, but just for very different reasons.

But back to the time and point in hand: not too long after the dream of being a policewoman had been crushed, the dream of becoming a plumber began to shine brightly. That dream, along with the promise of 250 big ones per week, was dead within minutes.

At the time, I still looked like Buzz McCallister, but I wasn't American or rich; I was kind of having a tough time in school because ... well, *see an accurate description of self above*, and my gran was trying to get me to go out with a 16-year-old painter and decorator even though he was morbidly obese and sweated pushing the high buttons in the lift.

I decided to give Fat Frodo the old swerve, and not because I thought I was better than him, but because it was a dead cert that the peer abuse would double, and so I started thinking about getting my own trade so my gran would stop trying to set me up with tradies in her area so she could get free things, like her living room papered and her toilet unclogged.

Sometimes dreams don't come true.

When Big Max heard the news, her immediate reaction was one of confusion: 'So, wait – you're telling me I've spent the past 14 years telling you that you can be anything you want and you want to be a plumber?'

I gave her a little nod-shrug to indicate my certainty. 'It's that or I have to go out with Fat Frodo from Gran's block!'

She ignored the last part of what I'd said steadfastly.

She got up in a non-threatening manner and went and pulled the plunger out from under the kitchen sink. She handed it to me and said, 'Wait outside the bathroom until Adam (he's my stepdad) comes out. He had a curry last night.' After that, I realised that plumbers are actually underpaid and not overpaid, as had previously been my assumption.

I wasn't wavering, I definitely didn't want to be a plumber anymore, but if I hadn't been put off then, there was an incident not too much later that would definitely have cured my wants. My mate Craig's dad was a plumber, and Craig wanted to be one, too. One day, Craig's dad got so drunk that he couldn't respond to a callout, and so three of us – myself, Craig and our mate, Sean – showed up in his place. We were at this quiet little house at the back of Fintry in Dundee, where a sweet old lady opened the door to us.

She showed us to her bathroom, after which she didn't seem that sweet anymore.

A plunger wasn't cutting it. I don't know what they feed OAPs, but they might want to chuck in a bran flake and a prune every now and then.

We didn't want to let his dad down, and we didn't want Craig's dreams to be dashed, so when he ordered one of us (obviously me) to go and ask for a potato masher, what else could I do?

I told him to fuck off. But did offer the conditioner as a potential contender.

A solution was gotten to in the end. That's all we'll say about it.

Everything else I wanted to be – from astronaut, vet, psychologist, sociologist, zoologist, teacher, inventor, scientist, researcher, actor, dancer, designer, architect, therapist, producer, painter, radio host, truck driver and Olympian to marathon runner – was supported by Big Max.

Extortionist was also supported, because her biological grandfather was the first man to 'gain' money from the post office, thanks to his inherent talent for forgery.

I went on to be a cleaner. Then I sold some shoes, cleaned some more, worked a few bars, sold some stolen stuff, worked as an optical assistant, applied and was denied the opportunity to become a Disney princess in Paris, and worked in a nursery, which I had to vacate via the window of the staffroom because of crippling regret and fear and more regret, before finally working offshore as an ROV pilot – all of which Big Max supported.

Since then, I've had a few other interests, like stunt work and modelling, but there aren't sufficient glove and balaclava gigs to thrive in the latter, and I don't like injuries enough for the former.

I was a pilot for a while, and then I married my boss. I'm a hacker for the most part now, and my own boss, so I'm snookered, because you can't marry yourself for half the money and 1% of the work.

Since I was about six years old, Big Max has said I should be a writer. I never did it because I don't like to be told what to do, but now is different because I'm doing it to spite her.

Cue seven-year-old me's love song:

In my
Dreams tonight

In ma dreams tonight
i saw you & i,
& we were hand & hand
dancing round the sky
so come with me
to a wonder land
were weel be free
so free i can feel the
magic bowring over me
so come with me to a
wonder land to take ma
hand and weel be happy
weel be greats to
gether & to this
wonder land

M. Reynolds
(PeSP)

I know, a prodigy walks among us. It is I.

8. You'll go in a home

Sadly, this turned out to be wishful thinking for us both.

The idea of a home – a beacon of light sparkling off in the distance, like a newly opened Butlin's – filled me with unadulterated, unbridled joy nine times out of ten; I was quite sure I'd love it there.

You'd be living with your mates and outnumber the adults. What's not to like?

I remained a wee bit wary about it all because she'd said something about there not being jailbroken cable boxes, but on the whole, I was pretty enthusiastic.

Our relationship was on the rocks because she was telling me what to do a lot and I was doing the opposite.

'Max, don't die!'

'Mum, don't tell me what to do! God, you're ruining my life!'

It was all very one-sided, so I started spreading the word among my friends that there was a place where children could go to get away from their parents, like a holiday camp, but without all the negativity of the parents wishing they were en route to Marbella instead of singing 'The Wheels on the Bus' and thinking up new ways to kick the bejesus out of the camp mascot.

We all seemed pretty up for it. One of my childhood best mates, Tracey, started helping me persuade the rest of the kids on the landing to get onboard, but the dream was taken from us too soon.

Lying is not a victimless crime and Big Max was just as sad as me when it all came tumbling down. Sadder maybe.

One day she shouted at me for losing my socks and not listening again. This resulted in me packing my bags, which were heavy-duty plastic bags from Farm Foods that I kept under my bed for emergencies – the same bags I'd originally planned on using as a raincoat and matching swimming cap if I ever ran away.

In them I packed two pairs of floral-print pants and one Disney pair, two T-shirts, a pair of Le Coq Sportif track pants, a Take That CD, my E17 book, and my bike pump, and then I took myself and the bags downstairs and told her I was going to the children's home, but wondered if she could just give me the address and a rough set of hand-directions.

The negotiations started with her asking me why I wanted to go there. I kept up the pretence that I just wanted to check it out and that she shouldn't be too upset.

My first mistake was letting her know I was chuffed at the prospect of going. My second was not lying my way out of the first fast enough.

Turns out there is no kids' holiday camp in Scotland, and possibly none exist in the entire world. Naturally, I was riddled with disappointment. I'm still unsure if I've made a full recovery.

My Spidey-senses told me it was too good to be true at the time, but I had no choice but to push those feelings deep, deep down into the cracks of my broken soul.

Jokes. I believed it all fully.

What made it worse was the release of *Harry Potter*. I lived in hope for half a decade that I just missed my Hogwarts letter because we didn't have a chimney.

Being a kid is great if you think about it. You don't have to fact-check a fucking thing and people lie to you for the better – Christmas as an example. WHOPPER. Tooth fairy? Definitely thought up by paedophiles. Easter? Someone really fat thought that up and I salute them.

And yet all you have to do is believe, which makes it true. And then lie about believing it all when some other child looking to free you from the grip of denial tells you Santa's 100% dead, etc.

Guiding tip: Believe nothing they tell you and everything you want for a happier life. Also, don't tell them your happiest thoughts; they will take them from you.

9. Being a parent is a thankless task (the story of the birthday miracle)

Well, it was clear from the off that I certainly wasn't going to thank the salty bi*ch. I should really have been the one being thanked for undergoing her questionable parental tactics. Alas, it just wasn't to be.

It was also proof there's no god and that we don't choose our family.

One time, though, I made a blunder: I responded out loud to the insult.

'Being a parent really is a bastarding thankless task,' she'd huffed aloud, punctuating the hateful statement with the death stare (at me).

'Well, I didn't ask you to have me! If I'd have known that I was coming out to you, trust me, I'd have stayed in there and choked myself with the cord,' was the comeback no less!

I mishandled the situation.

It was too long. It was too advanced. It was too dark for this world.

You know when you were younger and an adult would say something arsehole-y and you'd reply under your breath with an 'OKAY!' laced with attitude and resentment, and then they'd say, 'What did you just say?' And with clenched cheeks, you'd have to lie and say something like, 'I said, "Look! The cat's being gay!"' And nine out of ten times they'd let it pass? Yeah, that didn't happen this time.

My eyes, without hesitation, began to dart around looking for routes of escape but, in doing so, briefly caught the dead-still faces and glares of all the other adults in the room. I think my aunt Jenny was looking at the TV, but with her eyes closed. My other two aunts were looking at the floor and ceiling respectively but no longer seemed to be breathing.

My support group was once again letting me down.

I, myself, was still looking for an alternative to the body slam I'd just earned. I had one choice: the pelvis tuck, or, for the cool kids, the 'pelvuck'. It's where you haul in your ass, pull your pelvis up towards your belly button and then jog forward, away from the danger, in a bid to lower the risk of being kicked up the arsehole.

But, somehow, it turned out to be one of those mysterious, miraculous, magical times when nothing violent transpired. Instead, a rather glorious short few moments followed – she laughed.

This, my 13th birthday, turned out to be the day of two miracles. The first was the one just described. While the rest of us looked on hoping that her reaction to my insult wouldn't be so grievous that someone would have to call social services, my mum burst into fits of laughter and chortled out, 'Yep, you're your mother's daughter.'

Darkness.

A deep sense of anguish and despair filled the pit of my stomach when she confirmed that we were definitely related.

Blackness developed and stayed. All hope of a 'Happy 13th birthday – wooohooo! You're adopted' fell away, and I was left bereft of all happiness, which was added to in the absence of any word from Hogwarts.

However, that was the only laugh she afforded herself that night. For the rest of it, her face looked like her mouth was sucking a lemon, and her words were just as bitter. Thankfully, she left me at my aunt's house that night, in what can only be described as a miracle of grand proportions – the second of the day – resulting in a much-needed break from the heinous tyranny she called *parenting*.

This was also the year she would buy me a guinea pig and refuse to let it out of its cage, then harangue me for the animal seeming depressed, then get rid of it on my behalf.

She wasn't all that bad, though: one time she let me keep the stray dog I brought home for a whole hour. But then it sh*t on the carpet, and with one look she had me take it back to the outside to live alone.

But I'd stolen it from its tied location on the fence next to the shop, so it was probably for the best.

Guiding tip: Avoid eye contact when dishing out verbal insults. Look scared if they hear you. When they ask you to repeat what you just said, think of something that rhymes.

Birthdays were great when you were younger. Your mates' parents made them come to your party just so you'd be obliged to go to theirs, making none of us unpopular. You'd have a countdown. The bigger the badge, the cooler you were. If you got cranky, everyone just said it was because you'd had a long day and people had to be nice to you. It's all downhill after age 12.

MIRACLES HAPPEN EVERY DAY. If they don't happen for you, pretend your life is worse than it is and then re-examine for said miracles.

10. Move your shit or I'll throw it out!

Remember when you used to be two seconds from a psychotic breakdown because your mum moved your things? You know what's worse? Worse than Trump's wall, worse than your mate putting petrol in your diesel engine? It's when your mum throws your things out because she bought you too many things.

It's a bit like cleaning the house before you set it on fire – you bought them, bish. Why don't we just set your purse on fire?

It's also a crucial blow to the creative juices when you're looking for a Super Soaker to pretend you're American with, and your mum tells you she's thrown it out.

Now, let's say you're a parent and that you agree with this tactic. First of all, you're wrong, and second of all, you're a really terrible person – no offence though.

When this ridiculous phrase started its recurring role in our exchanges, my usual response was, 'Wow! Calm down, Max. Are they finally accepting monopoly money at Toys R Us?'

And when I got older and the threat was made against articles of clothing and other precious pieces of my self-esteem, I usually responded, 'You told me last week I'm not allowed a paper round because of "paedophiles", which kinda puts a new Kappa tracksuit out of my budget, so put that one the fuck down, Maxine!'

Note that what you just read is more or less the gist of what I responded, but there would have been no swearing, no recounting what she'd told me the week before because she'd already know what she said, and there would have been a clean STI test's chance in Charlie Sheen's house that I'd have managed to utter a single syllable before being the beneficiary of a Boston crab. But I was definitely, definitely thinking it.

Source: Wikipedia.

An accurate depiction of a Boston Crab

She really did do it, though; every once in a while, she made good on the threat and threw my toys out, and usually right in front of me. You've never experienced trauma like watching Barbie go down the bin chute at the same time as the tomato ketchup.

11. You're out of here the minute you hit 16!

If I could count high enough to describe how many times I heard, 'You're out on your ass the day you hit 16. Your attitude stinks!', I'd be a maths professor at Harvard with a side degree in Bullshit Judging.

Guiding tip: Leave home at age 15 like me to really throw them off their game.

Other things said in our house (and elsewhere)

Tell the bus driver you're four

I was four years old until I was about seven and a half. My mind was probably about that of a seven-year-old, and my height was about that of a 12-year-old, but my bus fare remained that of the under-fives: free.

One day, right after she'd shouted at me for being alive, we were on our way out, presumably to go somewhere less depressing.

I remember thinking her screeching was greatly uncalled for – it was something to do with things going in one ear and out the other, I don't recall because I wasn't listening. She'd been starting to get really repetitive.

The bus came after what felt like an eternity of standing gloomily at the bus stop on Princes Street, hoping someone walking by was out and about and ready to adopt (in the theatre of destruction that showcased my life, it wasn't to be).

When we got onto the bus, she said to the driver, 'Full fare for me, and she's under five.'

He looked at me. Dave was his name, which I knew because, like all four-year-olds, I could read like I belonged in Mensa.

He looked at what was surely an extremely tall, precocious infant and asked, 'How old are you, pal?'

I played my part well.

I gleefully replied, 'Seven, but she told me to say four. Thanks, Dave.' Then, victoriously, I took my seat on the bus.

Luckily Dave laughed.

But then Dave kicked us off the bus.

Dave could've let it go, but Dave was a fucking jobsworth.

Get fucked, Dave. No one likes a bus driver who thinks the fares come out of their pay. Unless the fares do come out of your pay, in which case, we are all really sorry.

Big Max was also not that chuffed. She squeezed on my arm tighter than speedos around Peter Kay's booty and whisper-shouted at me as we got off that bus, which is really no way to treat a four-year-old.

We walked into the town with one of us seething and the other one of us dreading quiet traffic periods.

Guiding tip: Lie when they want you to; lie when they don't want you to.

I don't care what your friends are allowed to do. They've obviously got shitty parents!

This delightful saying, sure to get her a few more mates in Dundee, was usually brought out to metaphorically body-slam me anytime I wanted to:

1. Stay out as late as my friends.
2. Go out as early as my friends.
3. Go to any street other than the one my aunt lived on.
4. Go to a place that my mother couldn't see from our four-up flat that looked out onto a car park.
5. Attend a sleepover.

When I got older:

1. Stay out as late as my friends.
2. Go somewhere that wasn't as close as three streets north, south and west of my aunt's house. I also wasn't allowed more than one street east because that was Kirkton, and bad things happened in Kirkton. She was adamant that although 'there are good people in Kirkton', I wouldn't be lucky enough to stumble into one of them. Instead, I'd find 'a crackhead

who'd take my money and give me a squint-eye'.
3. Attend a sleepover.
4. Go anyplace other than the ice rink and the cinema.

But as I got older, I got a little bit better at outwitting her. I say outwitting... it might have been down to pure luck.

Ah, gone are the days when you used to tell your parents you were ordering pizza and practising the recorder when you were actually dying in a field from too much stolen Russian vodka. Those were the good ole days, weren't they?

There was this one time ('*at band camp*') when I'd strategically planned out how I was going to get to the carnival – the carnival that came to town but once a year, and the carnival I was banned from ever going to. She was merciless and of the unwavering opinion that 'paedos go to carnivals'.

The plan I had concocted relied heavily on the public buses running on time to get me to the stop outside of the Ice Arena and close to my gran's house, as well as my mum relying heavily on my gran to make sure I was home on time.

One half of that *competent* plan was carried out with such adroitness that I actually couldn't have planned it – the public buses did indeed run on time. A Scottish miracle to be sure!

But that, as you might have guessed, is where the miracle ended its journey.

My mum thought that she would check up on me that particular weekend, deciding that my gran would definitely not be the one to make sure I was home on time and sober.

In a massive plot twist, instead of just waiting at my gran's for me to show up on time, Big Max herself made sure that I was indeed at the ice skating arena as I should be on a Saturday night.

She walked up there from my aunt's house in the Charleston area of Dundee. Unlike the other aunt, whose house I frequented, this aunt was heavily on my mum's side, and I always felt she liked to watch me have my ass handed to me for things like breathing too loudly or accidentally getting pregnant at 16 – a story for another time.

So, Dundee's version of Thelma and Louise, only more violent and without a car or a driving licence between them, and with me as their only target, made their way to the Ice Arena. Who were they ferociously scanning the bustling crowd of teens outside the ice rink for? Me. And who did they find? Me. So what was the issue, I hear you cry? Well, Big Max took one look at my squint-eye shaking under the pressure and my nerve rash spreading its way from my Pod boots to my neck and knew I was up to something not in line with her rules. Either that, or Jesus was back again.

So what option was I left with? Where would I say I'd been? Well, obvz I'd say I was at the cinema, which was right next door.

You're thinking what I was thinking: TOP PLAN. I'd nailed it.

I had not nailed it.

It was not a top plan.

Lie-Hound Reynolds sniffed that shit-nugget before it had even fully passed my little lie-spouting lips. She walked me into the cinema and asked the first employee she met what time *Crossroads*, the Britney Spears movie, had ended.

The employee replied (like there was, in fact, a God and I was warmly basking in His favour), 'Ten minutes ago, I think.'

Yesssssssssssssssss!

Waaaaay!

Ee-zee!

Boooooooom!

Shabbaaaaa!

Teckle!

Get it up you!!!

Get to f*ck, Big Max. I have won. I am the new overlord.

Today was not the day, I repeat, **not the day** I was going to make her day and give her something to really rim me for.

Part of me, and it wasn't a small part, wanted to hug that guy in a bear grip so strong that his braces popped off.

That was until something truly heinous ensued: the beginning of my own personal 9/11. Having no one look at him, face him, see him, wonder about him, know about him, think about him, care about him, watch him, ask about him, acknowledge him or want him in their general vicinity, this other smug, priggish-looking, erratically skinned little prick approached from the far left in order to let both Thelma and Louise know that *Crossroads* wasn't playing at all that sad, sad, soon-to-be-sore-arsed night.

I argued with him. Obviously.

I didn't have any at the time, but if I had, I would have argued my tits off with him.

I was like, 'Look, sir, it was playing. I was in there, and it was playing and I know that it was playing because I was in there and the only way I'd be in there knowing that it was playing is if I was in there and it was playing. And I was. So ... Okay, well, glad we got that cleared up.'

Inside my head I was like, *I'm winning this. I can outsmart him. He's a popcorn maker!*

Nope. He was a smart popcorn maker.

After some back and forth, he banged out the deathblow and called the manager over.

This was getting bananas.

Now, people, I know my limits; I know how much I am willing and able to suffer, and I know when I need to back down to reduce the upcoming sentence.

I flitted round in one rapid movement, put on my 'I'm terribly sorry I disobeyed you' face and started to declare my deceit, the moral burden of it, and went on to talk briefly about how much I'd wanted to tell her the truth long ago.

And, yeah ... No, she didn't take it well.

I knew it wasn't going in my favour when she uttered the words, 'Why didn't you just *ask* to go to the carnival?' in a light, airy, ice-queen tone.

She knew how that game of verbal chess went, and she knew I wasn't yet functioning enough like an adult not to take the bait, so when, without further ado, I said the obvious – 'Because you wouldn't let me' – her eyes narrowed and the corners of her mouth stretched upwards, indicating that she knew I was, indeed, a little bastard.

Trying to trick me into thinking I might be able to sit on my arse again sometime the following week, she said in a very delicate, but vaguely sinister, voice, 'So, you knew I wouldn't let you go?'

I replied, 'Yeah', but in a kind of whisper that could hopefully be misheard and made to sound like any response that was the right one.

'So you lied, and you got other people to lie for you!' Her creepy, 'I'm about to rim you' voice started creeping in about this point. 'How do you know that spotty little lying bastard in there?' (Referring to the virtuous although lackadaisical employee who thought that damn Britney Spears movie was still playing.)

Anyway, thanks to Thelma, Louise and that needy prick, whose face looked like it had banged a deep-dish pizza, outmanoeuvring me, I got grounded for a month and had to call Big Max from the ice rink's payphone every half hour for the following six months so she could make sure that I was really there.

Did you know that a teenager's brain isn't yet formed like an adult's? They may look like spotty grown-ups, but they have more grey matter and are neurobiologically inclined to be little dick tips.

The odds were never in my favour to begin with. Big Max was the Kevlar of parents. She was pretty sure I was going to be murdered or molested, or worse: drunk. There was a lot I wasn't allowed to do. The carnival was at the very top of that list. The rest of the list was also comprised of normal teen activities.

Guiding tip: Say the word 'neurobiology', followed by 'sorry', when in trouble. Watch the parent crumble. Unless you have a neurobiologist for a parent, in which case you're f*cked and not in any good way.

Just a thought, right ... Do you ever wonder how your parents got away with things when they were younger and how the times change from one generation to the next? Like, what lies did they have to tell to stay out later, how did they steal penny farthings and how did their parents check on them, find out they were being little bastards and then backhander them?

It's also a bit strange to think that, back in the day, your grandad's next-door neighbour was allowed to drop-kick him if he was a little dick, whereas nowadays you'd have old Bert banged up and tagged as a child abuser before the bruise had formed.

I don't know which environment is best insofar as what was allowed back then and what's allowed today, but let's assume we aren't going backwards and try to picture what it'll be like for future generations given the current trajectory … So, as far as I'm aware, it's now frowned upon for parents to sucker-punch their kids, so it's definitely a no-go for the neighbour to dish out the wedgies and whatnot. What if all the abuse stops and then in 20 years all we have is a generation of Donald Trumps, but poor. Not ideal, is it?

But then, on the other hand, what if we were all walking about choke-holding other people's kids? Also not favourable conditions.

Let's all stop having kids and get dogs. No one can hit another person's dog. Bugsied.

If you don't know what 'bugsied' means, GET OUT!

You know what
must be really, really
sh*t about being a
parent?
You can't put
something in the
microwave
and then have everyone
eat around the hard,
semi-frozen bit in the
middle.
That's a pre-parent
sport.

It *is* vegetarian

The backdrop for this cluster-fuck was my mum's temporary house while she and my stepdad were on a prolonged 'relationship vacation'.

It was in a little place that used to be known as 'Emergencies-only Charleston'.

I was getting ready to leave for my first job as a pilot over in Norway. Someone had told me that Norway seemingly had a lot of vegetarians.

'I was a vegetarian for years!' I mused out loud, my voice filled with smugness, such is the voice of any vegetarian or vegan. 'Remember when I was a veg gangsta, mum?'

She wasn't in my eyeline because I was sat on the floor looking over the lies I'd jotted down on my CV. (Come on, we all tell white lies on our résumés.)

I couldn't see why she wasn't responding, so I just continued.

'Would you say I was a level nine vegetarian?' I asked, pretty much talking to myself. 'I was never going to be a ten. I had that hotdog when we went to Blackpool.'

I actually was vegetarian from about age eight until age 14, so level nine was deserved.

Or was I?

She fed me dead animals for the entire duration and paraded it as Quorn, which is a delicious meat substitute. Or is it? I don't know because I've never tasted it!

Never has a more gullible person lived. When I saw her put actual sausages on my plate, I would be like, 'Those heart-clogging cylindrical meat parts aren't the Quorn ones you put on the *other side* of the grill for me!', with a tone akin to 'get your shit together, woman. Stop trying to poison me.'

It was like taking part in an at-home pantomime. She'd be like, 'Oh no I didn't', and I'd be at the kitchen table saying back, 'Oh yes you did, you c*nt!', but on the inside.

There were a few times I'd note that the sausages were identical and say it to her: 'Mum, are these real sausages, because yours looks almost identical to mine?'

She'd say they were definitely Quorn, and sometimes she'd mix it up and tell me they were Linda McCartney. My eyes would fill up in gratitude, and, wiping my thankful tears away while thinking about all the animals we were saving, I'd give her thanks and watch her face light up in ~~love~~ betrayal.

Back to her bachelorette pad a short ten years later, and it wasn't until she just about sh*t her skirt laughing at me that I found out about the whole sordid affair in all of its treacherous detail. I was not and never had been a vegetarian. I'd rather watch Simba die on repeat than see how gleeful this made her.

So, just as my cocoon (aka Scotland) released me like a wide-eyed butterfly at the ripe age of 19 years old, she told me that I could stop bragging about being a vegetarian to anyone who would listen. I, in fact, had eaten more sausage than a German prostitute.

Act sorry?

Hahahahahaha!

No.

She couldn't have been less contrite if she was the entire cast of *Chicago* in one woman. She laughed so hard that day, we had to ice her jaw then massage it for an hour.

It fell off the back of a lorry (truck)

Like all good mothers, mine strived to make what parts of my life she wasn't bound to make absolute hell good, comfortable and starvation-free, so with these fundamentals in mind, she would often acquire things like coats, shoes and food, including 'Quorn', 'off the back of a lorry'.

I asked her what else we got, and, well, we're all sorry, Asda!

Oh, lots of stuff! ███ had a shop lifter go into ███ once a week with bag of stuff! There was always meat, cheese, coffee, bacon, clothes, shampoo! Everything really. Xxxxxxxx

Why? What do you need to know for? 😏

I'm going to see a man about a dog! (And he was always 'sold out')

I don't believe I'm taking jack-shit out of context when I tell you that she could easily have been mistaken as a drug dealer ... by me.

Is there any other reason to leave the house at 10 p.m. every night, saying, 'I'm going to see a man about a dog'? The dead giveaway was obviously that we never got a dog. We didn't even pat strangers' dogs.

I recently found out that she was going to work. Her job was as a doorman at a club called De Stihl's in Dundee, whereby her job description offered her the rare opportunity to wrestle men.

I would 100% be willing to set up a fight between Big Max and Ronda Rousey. There's a strong chance she'd die, but there's also a solid chance I'd be rich after that, and then Ronda would be my mum.

Guiding tip: Believe nothing.

POLICE OFFICER:

Turn around!

In Scotland:

US AS PEDESTRIANS:

Bright eyes!

(The five million of us are pretty cool.)

That time I ran away and the police brought me home

'That's it! We are moving to England!' She'd said it using the edge of her voice.

I'd run away to my friend's house and hidden in her mum's attic. Why I hid is beyond me – I'm pretty sure Fritzl could've camped in Patsy's loft. As teens, we thanked her profusely for the glorious gift of letting a gaggle of rowdy teens use her house like a delinquent teen camp.

Anyway, my mum and stepdad came to get me, and I got scared and jumped out the back window ... one flight up. I hurdled the back fence and ran to Clatto Country Park.

Adam, my stepdad, was a heavy smoker and would have been out of breath grating cheese, and my mum's midget legs could only turbo her so far, so the glory was mine for a wee while at least.

I outpaced them both and took a victory lap around the pond. Soon after the escape, I disappeared.

Jokes.

I made the massive error of returning to the scene of the crime.

By then the police had shown up. It was great. Wish I could relive that day ...

I was escorted home in the back of a comfortable and luxurious car decorated with metal window coverings and child locks on the doors, not to mention an engraving on the back of the leather seat that read 'Fuck you! Die, pig', staring me in the face all the way home.

But the path to our house was lit by the warm glow of the cosy interior and all the love that awaited me inside. The garden was lined with rose bushes that scented the air, and I almost fell to my knees thinking about how sorry I was and what I'd do to take it all back ...

Lies.

I had to be dragged up the four flights of stairs to our flat and forced through the front door by the policeman's foot. I even told them that if they took me home, they'd be the accomplices to my death, because I was sure Big Max was going to murder-punch me within the first 28 seconds of entering.

They did not care. They walked me to her like I was Ned Stark.

Cue the violence.

I attacked her. That's right. 'Twas I who started this one. My bad, guys, my bad. Seemed warranted at the time.

I mishandled the situation.

Hormones are a real and proper struggle.

After years of being clouted, drop-kicked, held upside down and beaten like a drum, held up the right way round and beaten like a drum, and hit with hairbrushes like a human piñata, I went at her like I was Gerard Butler in *300*.

Although, in hindsight, if I think about it carefully, it was probably an absolute blunder. It was likely the one time she wasn't going to own me.

Not ideal timing.

Instead of viewing her lack of violence as a truce, I saw a window to assert my dominance. And that's how I came to lose my front tooth, have no dignity and have no dominance.

I thrust at her, feet first. Puberty, hormones and hatred propelled me through the air at a near-perfect feet-first angle, and, upon contact, the machines attached to me from the hip down started rotating like I was Lance Armstrong doing the Tour de France. Got seven good kicks in ... was pretty dope.

I could've gone on like that for hours. Didn't break a sweat. I could've snacked, continuing to turbo-hoof Big Max in any and all body parts she put in my way. Sadly, I was quickly prohibited from doing so.

She found my weakness in seconds: the rest of my body.

Turns out that for a 5′ 4″ woman, she has long arms. They looked like two pythons that had swallowed a bag of ropes, and they weren't bound by the same natural laws as the rest of humankind. She grabbed my stick arms; hoisted me up, leaving my machine-legs dangling downward, lame under the full exertion of gravity;

and swung her face so close to mine I could see the vein throbbing in her forehead.

We disagree on the finer points from here on in. But she definitely headered me.

My tooth hit off of her forehead. Then it fell out.

PING! Then a little *clack!* Then a little searching the floor to hopefully see any other body part ... like maybe a nail. Then a lot of crying.

Things that happened immediately after:
1. The tooth was put in milk.
2. She ran to the phone box to phone my aunt and tell her what she'd done (we hadn't paid our phone bill that month).
3. She returned and grounded me for two goddamn months!
4. I cried again and asked her why she couldn't have broken my nose instead.
5. She said I was to go to my room and not come out until we went to the dentist in the morning.
6. In the morning, she said I was to say it was someone else's head entirely that had removed my tooth from its home at the front of my mouth.
7. She really kept me grounded for two months.

Ah, Big Max, how we laugh about it now, now that I've got both front teeth and so don't whistle when doing so.

Guiding tip: If you want an adrenaline hit, just throw your bath mat out. Your mum will probably always own you in a fight.

I'm not scared to put you on your arse in front of anyone, dear!

Fear – a harrowing yet result-driven tactic.

Describe fear for us, Max! I hear you all say.

Okay, I will.

I hang-glide. I box with a man who could knock out King Kong mid-rage. I can fly planes. I've been great white shark diving and I've looked at my bank account after a long weekend. I know fear.

There's no fear more striking and crippling than that imposed by your mum.

One year at Christmas, Big Max physically walloped me body-wide for not saying the words 'thank you' loud enough. It's nice to unclench your gifts instead of unwrapping them.

A *#GiftsNotFists* hashtag should be started immediately for kids everywhere who bear the brunt of parents that've been saving for seven months straight for things they've now got to build and buy batteries for.

I should've seen it coming, given that we had the same fight each and every year, without fail (I use the term 'fight' loosely, because it was just me on the ground in a foetal position and her telling me to stay still).

Another year my stepdad walked into the kitchen as I was receiving my very last – *ahem* – 'gift' for the festive period and walked back out.

The Overlord had struck again – literally. We were all scared of her and I don't know why. What we should've done was to band together as a family, tie her up and walk her through City Square like what happened to Cersei in *Game of Thrones*.

When I was younger, I thought my mum Bobby Browned me through my childhood because I was the smallest, the weakest and plausibly the most afraid of her. And there's a good chance that's exactly what it was, because she didn't batter Adam when he annoyed her.

But in all seriousness, I think parents who hit their kids do so because they don't know what else to do.

Big Max was pretty quick to anger most of her teens, 20s, 30s and 40s, and she just wanted me to listen. But what she could've started with were the words, 'Max, I just want you to listen …'

The irony is this: I bet you 10,000,000 Iranian dollars that if I have kids and even breathe on them too heavily, she would put me in a chokehold and then a coma.

Guiding tip: It's like a party piece: you pretend like you don't want to scissor-kick the kid, and you just have a glass of wine. Or two. Or three. Or however many you can have and still make it to bed. The time of day should not be an indicator of how good an idea this tip is. Just crack open the bottle instead of your kid.

When I read her this section in an effort to both fact-check and make her feel momentarily worthless, she said, 'I wasn't punching you! Take that out!'

To which I replied, 'Uhhhhh, yes you were!'

'I wasn't, Max!' she whinged back in protest. 'Adam wouldn't have let me,' she insisted, with her chest puffed and brows almost meeting one another in the middle of her forehead. 'Maybe,' she continued in an alarmingly familiar tone indicative of faux calm, 'I just had my hands around your throat *gently* …'

Everyone clap for Big Max. Without her, who knows, I could be out of control, giving your son AIDS or something terrible like that … or way less knowledgeable about veneers.

I've got mates who have the same issues – parents conveniently forgetting things that should definitely not be forgotten.

Step aside, Turkey Necks, we remember.

I'm not scared to put you on your arse in front of anyone, dear! (in front of a police officer)

This is tried and tested. Take one guess as to who won ...

If you bet on her, well, more fool you, suckers. Her arsehole could've knitted a jumper. It was glorious to see and shall stay with me until death.

This particular time, I could tell she was seething as I lay on the cold, chewing-gum-decorated ground outside of RS McColl's at the Ardler shops for no real reason, because when she told me to get up, her voice sounded like one that'd tortured James Bond.

After the short stand-off in front of a police officer's curious, very unwanted eyes, she lowball growled that she would have words with me later, although she held my arm tight enough to sever it.

This particular saying taught me that, contrary to popular opinion relayed to me by my friends, family, peers and basically anyone who wasn't in the police force in Dundee, and one man who was, a policeman's environment was a safe environment and one that was violence-free.

Another 'amusing' example

After nearly nine months in which I hadn't seen her, Big Max finally made it to Miami. After some wishful thinking, she touched down as expected and the Sunshine State seemed a little more dull.

Obviously, I'm joking. I had a ceremony for her coming and everything. I'd missed her. I'd forgotten! Time had played its cruel tricks again and my mind was blissfully, but temporarily, unaware that we can't help but fight after day two together. Plus, I'd just moved there for work with the man who'd one day become my ex-husband, and I couldn't fob her off anymore.

We hadn't lived together for about six years at this point, so, as you can imagine, it was great and went swimmingly when she stayed with me for three weeks ... That's the end of this story.

Except it's not and I never hated her more.

So, raise your hand if you know of a single other person in the world who can annoy you quicker than you own mum ... (*Imagines arenas full of people sitting on hands.)

I'll tell you the one word that was needed for the Miami population to think Scarface had made a return to South Beach: 'lazy'.

Accidentally on purpose, in one small breath and with half a second of eye contact, I called her lazy.

Spitting bare truths since '88. Ha. Kidding. I've got to say that because she may still have it in the old hip flexer to HACHA! me.

She did not take it how I meant it, though. Well, she took it exactly how I meant it, but I just thought it'd slip by her.

Negative. She went ballistic.

To stop her screaming at me in front of my very new, very taciturn boyfriend, who just about went foetal rather than witnessing it, I had to tell her I'd call the police. Big Max turned white underneath her two-week tan. It was a sight to behold. It looked like her blood had turned to ice, no longer too enthusiastic about its job of keeping her alive.

She used to watch the BBC news, so she knows they carry guns and that they hate people who look like they might be black. She snarled something about me being a 'hussy', of all things (like she'd completely forgotten the time I stopped Disabled Dave in the wheelchair from entering me), all because I'd started going out with my boss.

Happens.

Then there was something about how disappointed my gran would be in me (if she wasn't bat-shit nuts), and then she finished it off with a spectacular announcement about how the devil probably lived in me, before leaving.

She's only ever reacted like that once before. I was 14 years old, and as she was mid-caterwaul, shrieking about some phantom rule I'd broken, I ever so gently shrieked back that I was going to live with my dad. She went silent. Her breath caught like she'd just sharted. No sounds came out of her and she stayed dead still.

It was a joyous, beautiful sight. Like watching a sunset, actually.

The thing was, I hadn't seen my dad since I was three years old and Big Max had stolen me back after he'd kidnapped me for three months, moving houses in a bid to continuously outsmart her – which was also around about the time his girlfriend secretly burned my legs accidentally, but also accidentally twice. We do not like her. She was a hot-headed sort (see what I did there ...).

That whole last paragraph sounds a bit passive-aggressive, but not intentionally so. Gary did what he thought he should. He also didn't know his girlfriend was a monster.

Why let anyone else ruin your life when you're completely capable of doing it for yourself at any age.

#TalentsIWasBornWith

I've just always loved bad boys as is plainly captured here for all to see.

My gran and grandad before my gran went bat-sh*t nuts and started telling everyone he was a cross-dresser.

Big Max and all of my aunts looking good in their prime.

Big Max in her prime and in a time before filters. HUBBA HUBBA. (Don't make it creepy. She was hot.)

Me, when I looked like Honey Boo Boo's dad, and Big Max, when she looked like Jim Carrey.

My fivehead captured in all its glory. You're welcome. This is also mere days before all that saved Christmas was the Return and Refunds Law.

Bandits! My uncle and aunt at Leeds Festival. Me, probably drug-muling.

My auntie Jenny when Chanel's production was based in Turkey.

Big Max letting me know that burkas are all the rage. Steve, the coolest dog to have ever lived, thinks fur is still trending.

Two prime candidates for three years at a two-year college.

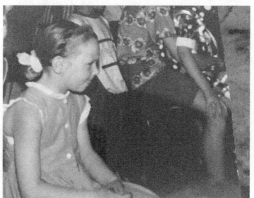

My thinking face, my angry face, my happy face, my cute face, my hungry face.

I like to think she's upset because she's holding a child that isn't me, but she just had really good resting bitch face. But she had a beauty that went down to her soul. NO YOU'RE GETTING EMOTIONAL JUST BECAUSE SHE'S GONE NOW! I don't know who the man in the back is, but he looks like a really thin Chandler.

INSPECTOR GADGET solves another mystery… How Big Max phones in sick to work (read on for full details and pointers).

She's not in blackface. She's asking, as I get ready for my wedding day, why I have blackface make-up …

"We live in the Kardashian-era, Big Max, what can I say?"

Being an adult
is really easy:
you just yell at
people younger than
you that you're tired.
Then tell people
your own age you're
tired and wait for
them to tell you the
same back.
Pretty much anyone
can do it.

Be! Because!

We'd been down to England to see my mum's dad. He was always chirpy and cheerful to me, but everyone – including himself – always said he was a miserable bastard.

Anyway, I was enjoying my time with him. We'd gone to the beach; we'd eaten out of the local chippy; we'd talked about how great a runner I was; we'd let me beat him in a sprinting match; and we'd talked about the importance of money, even though neither of us had any.

My mum was being kind of normal, too. On a scale of one to normal, she was sitting at around a *no-one-else-could-tell-she-was-off-her-rocker.*

She was also not actively trying to shit on my days from great heights, and she hadn't bitch-ploded in days. I felt as though my nine long years of life were finally on an upswing.

But then ...

'We' had a choice to make – head back to Scotland on the Wednesday or on the Thursday. I, of course, picked the Thursday, and she shrugged then decided that it wasn't such a bad idea. But when we tried to make the train on the Thursday, we missed it.

The devil was on the prowl in England that summer.

'We' slept in, even though one of us was up at 6 a.m. playing with her Polly Pocket toys. It was pretty much the exact same situation we'd been in when we were journeying down.

We headed to the train station anyway, but they told us we weren't getting home that day. Then she told me that it was my fault, like my side job as a preteen was scheduling the f*cking trains. Then she mocked me to my very face using her best and only interpretation of a little girl: she was all, *'Uhhhh, let's stay here! Let's go home on Thursday!'* With her arms flailing at her sides, too.

There was absolutely no f*cking way for me to tell if I really did talk like I was deaf or if it was just the way she was performing.

We'd gotten all the way back across London again and we'd still not heard the end of me making us miss the train. I decided to kill myself via Birds Eye and eat the leftover fish fingers from the night before. Something about the sight of a failed train scheduler eating a single pea at a time sent her over the edge and she hit the roof!

When she started shouting, I started storing a fish finger in each one of my cheeks, because when you're little, you know not to make any sudden moves. When she slapped me with her man-hand like a really evil Fat Controller, I *accidentally* spat fish fingers out over the kitchen. It looked like flaky snow scattering about the room.

To get to the point and to stop people from vomiting, she didn't take that well either. So, what we did was just not talk to one another for the next 12 hours.

We went to the train station the next day, and she bought me a colouring book and a set of colouring pens (read: guilt buy).

Soon after, we were arguing about how the pens should be used. There were two of each colour: one was a thin tip and the other was thick. 'Obviously,' she'd said, the thin tip was for going round the edges of pictures inside the book, and the thicker pen was to colour in the large area in the middle of 'whatever shitty thing' it was I was colouring.

Not this bish. This bish used one pen not only for the whole space, but for about three different shades, thanks to my command of pressure.

She said to me at some point, 'You aren't doing it the way it's supposed to be done! Why can't you just do it right?'

I started my answer without looking up at the devil's rep here on Earth. I was like, "Cause ...'

Finally, a situation handled like a boss.

But it turns out it doesn't matter where we are in the world; that woman will let me know if my grammar is crumbling faster than her patience. She immediately cut me off, stating that the word I was looking for was 'Be! Because', and if I couldn't talk properly, then I wasn't to talk at all.

That nine-hour train journey turned out to be a fricking dream. I didn't have to talk to her once. It remains one of my biggest victories against the one-woman Gestapo to date.

Guiding tip: Small wins count.

***

I really hope for most people that the stories in this book make you think about your own childhood.

Moreover, if some stories do act as a catalyst for remembering days gone by, hopefully it's the same for most as it is for me: looking back, it's all easily reframed as hilarious. The perceived horror of it at the time sort of fades into inconsequence. Maybe time is doing the heavy lifting, or maybe it's a mindset, I'm not sure. But, in any case being a parent seems like a lot of work with no discernible guidelines. You get one shot at being a kid. There's no way to get either experience right. There probably isn't a right. There's just the unfolding of time at a zero-distance range.

With all of that in mind, looking back and colouring the majority of childhood with our rose-tinted glasses seems innocuous.

Now, on with the jokes ...

I'm not here to be your friend!

Here's what happened: I'm not sure what I had done to deserve this extravagant ticket to freedom, but I was allowed to go to my friend Sammy's house one day after school, the likes of which happened so seldom I'm able to recall the details in all their glory.

Sammy lived quite far from where I lived at the time, but it was by my high school, so my mum and I agreed that I would go there after school and come home by 7.30 p.m., even though school finished at 3.25 p.m. and the bus ride home to our house was 40 minutes long. Still, I had just over three hours of glorious freedom ahead of me.

Kind of.

She said that I wasn't to leave Sammy's house under any circumstances. A rigid statement that demanded the question, 'Even if it's on fire?' She never answered it, and, given the tightrope I was walking towards freedom, I pushed the urge to deeply fuck her off by asking again deep, deep down.

Next, we come to how she was going to make sure I was keeping my end of the deal. You guessed it – by mobile phone.

I had a phone that was so big it actually did almost stop me leaving any house if I held it horizontally. It was so shit, it was akin to the tablet Moses carried, only it had Snake on it.

When she called it, we agreed that I was to take it to Sammy's mum so that she could confirm my location safely in her house and out of the reach of any mass murderers, sexual predators or fun.

This, of course, was not going to fit into my own plans. My friends and I had boys to be following about all night.

You know, it's funny, because looking back now, it was really a terrible yet hilarious mistake to convince myself that the reason boys in school weren't into me was because I wasn't allowed out late at night like the other girls.

It was a bit more likely/100% due to the fact I looked like Big Bird and my nicknames in school were 'Big Lips Wee Tits' and 'Manzie Kennels' (the latter because I looked like both man and dog, obviously).

Moving on: that bright, motherless night, I put on my creased tracksuit, which had been in my school bag and was, by that point, smelling faintly of the tuna sandwich I'd been given by the lunch lady that afternoon. I switched off my mobile so I could make my way my gaggle of teenagers without interference from Big Max. Naturally, we were nasty little bastards to one another, and the distinctive odour of warm tuna on my shell suit nearly ruined me.

They called me 'Fishy Kennels' for nearly three long weeks after that. But it seemed as though I was having a subtle stroke of luck: all of my mates went home early, so I didn't have to pretend I'd sprained my ankle.

After getting back to Sammy's, I tried, like any moronic teen, to make sure I hadn't been identified as a bad daughter in the eyes of Big Max.

I turned on the blue and silver Nokia hoping she'd forgotten my existence.

Apparently, the further you are from a parent, the more they think about you ... I had a text demanding I get home immediately. It was written in ALL CAPS, as if they were going to scare me more than regular-sized letters.

They did.

But I did, in fact, make it home with five minutes to spare.

Note: There are five levels of fear:
1. Panic
2. Terror
3. Missed calls from your mum
4. Texts in all caps from your mum
5. Thinking about how future-you is going to lie to your mum.

Enter the lie:
Timing just wasn't enough for Big Max. I'd broken our pact, and she'd not heard so much as one syllable from Sammy's mum. She'd only heard Nokia's voicemail. She asked where my phone was. I replied that I'd 'accidentally' left it at Sammy's

house and it had 'unbelievably and disturbingly in the extreme run out of battery earlier that day'. I gave my deepest, weightiest apologies for the whole 'unavoidable mishap' and offered her the chance to let it go.

Would she let it go?

'LOL' as the cool kids say. LOL. No. Never.

Cue the miraculous *feeling* that parents everywhere seem to be afflicted with whenever the mood strikes.

You know all my mum needed to know I'd been lying? Jesus. Except we don't believe in Jesus, which was the real miracle.

'I've got a feeling you're lying to me, Max.'

Before I knew it, I was shouting out of the living-room window to her (from four flights up over a busy main road), 'Why do you hate me?'

Any normal person would ignore the child frantically screaming out the window, or at least tell them to get back inside before they fell to their death. Not her. She turned and replied, 'Because I'm not here to be your friend!' and gave me the middle finger before turning back in the direction of the bus stop.

While she was on the first leg of her journey to Sammy's to check my ~~alibi~~ 'ali-lie' before returning to ruin my life, I panicked and ran to the phone box, dialled Sammy's number like I had Parkinson's and told her in no uncertain terms that she was to turn my phone on and off until the battery gave out, or, if that looked like it was going to take too long, she could do me a solid and burn her house down with the Nokia inside.

Thankfully, her house on Dalmahoy still stands.

You know what wasn't standing about two hours later? Me.

She decked me with precision. A ninja-cut to the back of the legs.

She then pivoted and positioned herself above me, so both she and the phone she was holding were in my line of sight. She was a little bemused as to how a phone that had run out of battery was able to be powered on and 'have three bars'.

'An Ardler miracle, Mum.'

She didn't believe in those. Just feelings.

I was never allowed back to Sammy's again because I was untrustworthy and too good at charging my phone.

Oh fucking really!

(Note: There are two people called Steven in this story.)

I was out on the landing of our tenement – minding my own business – when I was savagely attacked by my neighbour and his dad's hammer.

The little bastard got me right on the forehead. To be fair, it was a large target (look, you'd have a fivehead, too, if your eyebrows were albino).

Naturally, I ran home crying to my mum, which makes it sound like I'm a little bitch, but, in my defence, other people are shit.

When I threw myself past the front door and hurled myself crying, with just the right amount of histrionics most children develop over the course of a short amount of life, she, the always calm and placid mother of mine, spat out a menacingly laced, 'Oh fucking really!', and proceeded to advance up the hallway and run out of the house barefoot after Steven with a dish towel and the look of Hitler.

When she caught up with him, she wound the dish towel up and used it like the end of a hose.

But that wasn't enough for Big Max. Fraught with fear that her already weird child, just used like a human nail, might have been made weirder, she led Steven by the scruff of the neck to his mother's front door. As you might have guessed, it didn't turn out all that well for any of us.

The mother's door in question was only one down from our own, so I, like the rest of our neighbours, heard the whole thing by crouching in the hallway holding the letterbox open ever so slightly. I remember thinking there was a pretty sound chance she was going to have to bleach my back again, because young Steven was definitely not going to forget this.

The conversation between them ended like this:

Steven's mum: 'If you don't like the way my kid treats your kid, you'd better move!'

Big Max: 'Oh fucking really! Well, tell you what, I'm going to treat your kid exactly how he treats mine.'

Steven's mum: 'No, you won't! You'd better watch yourself, you jumped-up little c*nt.'

Big Max: 'Oh fucking really! Well, let me tell you this, Scurge, I'm going one better: I'm going to do to *you* everything that he does to my kid! And if you talk to me like that again, I'll smack the taste out of your fuc—' You get the point.

Steven's mother replied that Steven's dad would be along to see my mum and her boyfriend before the night's end. What can I say; we lived in a classy neighbourhood.

And so Big Max proceeded to wait in sour patience for the knocking of her door for the remainder of the night – the TV on mute, the living-room door open and her foot tapping like it had a twitch.

The door was indeed knocked on, that dark, swollen-headed night.

As I lay on the sofa with a warm towel round my head, feigning concussion so I wouldn't have to go to school the next day, Big Max got off the sofa like her bumhole was on fire and disappeared down the hallway like a bat going straight into the loving arms of hell.

She threw open the front door with such ferocity that a cold breeze flowed through the house, portending terrible things to come.

They came. Mist formed in the cold landings of Rosemount Road and three bars were turned up to four on fires the block over.

She filled her lungs and spoke about four octaves lower than any woman without chest hair should be able to.

The polite and respectable man standing at the front door had politely asked if Steven was there (also the name of my mum's boyfriend at the time), and he'd gotten a reply that was something along the lines of: 'No! You wanna talk about this, you talk to me! Come on then, what the fuck you got to say about it?'

My mum's opponent stared back at her, looking both concerned and distressed – not what you'd expect from a man who'd been sent along by his violence-enabling counterpart.

He took a little step back and put his palms up in the universal sign of surrender and asked once more for Steven ... his nephew.

The man who'd come to our door was, in fact, my mum's boyfriend's uncle, and, in a huge plot twist, he never came back to visit us again.

I think if Big Max had had one wish, she'd have used it right there and then to make the floor of our flat crack open, where there would have appeared a hole and a straight path down to the fiery depths of hell, a passage into which she would've immediately cannonballed.

I'm the adult and you're the child

One time, she threw away the frogs I'd 'captured' and kept in my aunt's backyard. One motherless summer's day, I'd made my way into Bridgefoot, Dundee's countryside, and collected some tadpoles with my two best friends at the time. We cycled everywhere together, and two of us always ganged up on one – always the most fun when you aren't the 'one'.

The time came in which the joyous news reached her joy-hating ears that my little green children had grown into beautiful croaking frogs. So, naturally, she tore them from their home since just after birth and put them back into their 'natural habitat'.

I didn't feel confident in her choice of home for them. I don't know where the niggling doubt came from, maybe I was just a child genius, but somehow I knew that they didn't belong in a somewhat deep puddle in the old railway station off Strathmartine Road. When I asked her (obviously from a distance) why she'd done that to me, and them, initially her answer was, 'Because I know best!'

Even at age 11, I knew that was some strong, hard, girth-y shite.

When she saw the lingering doubt pass over my face, she brought out the age-old, 'I'm the adult and you're the child' adage. And I knew my children would die along with my faith in adults.

Amen.

Guiding tip: Being an adult may only be that you're jaded and believe your own lies.

Cunningham's Law:
The best way to get a reaction and
the right answer
on the Internet
isn't to ask a
question, but to post
the wrong answer.
The same tactic
applies
to parents...

Give bad answers for the quick route to what they actually want to hear from you.

If your friends jumped off the bridge, would you?

Me: Ehhh, yeah! (I wasn't the sharpest tool in the box, but I was a good swimmer, so it probably would've worked out.)

Me: But all of my friends are getting tattoos!
Mum: If your friends jumped off the bridge, would you?

Me: But everyone else is allowed to go to Clatto Park!
Mum: My brother died there, and if your friends jumped off the bridge, would you?

Me: It's unfair! Everyone else is going to her sleepover!
Mum: If your friends jumped off the bridge, would you?

Me: But all my friends are going to the party!
Mum: If your friends jumped off the bridge, would you?

Me: But all of the other girls are allowed to drink alcohol!
Mum: If your friends jumped off the bridge, would you?

Me: But everyone else is wearing a padded bra!

Mum: If your friends jumped off the bridge, would you?

Me: But everyone else is wearing hoop earrings, and they don't look like hookers!
Mum: If your friends jumped off the bridge, would you?

Me: Every single girl my age in the whole of this city is allowed to wear a crop top and they don't all have 'shit parents'!
Mum: If your friends jumped off the bridge, would you?

Me: All the other girls are allowed to go to the under-18s disco!
Mum: If your friends jumped off the bridge, would you?

Me: If my friends ever make a pact to jump off that bridge, I'm doing it to prove a point!
Mum: You're an idiot.

Because I'm the adult and you're the child – part two

Alright, I'll give her this one. She, in what can only be described in the loosest of terms as an 'adult', was right. And I had to walk about like I could eat an apple through a tennis racket for years. Cue the year of no braces.

This day started out like not that many others: she was being nice to me straight off the bat. She let me watch Cartoon Network on the cable box we'd paid 40 quid to Dave for.

Everybody in Scotland knew a Dodgy Dave back then – he could literally get you a Corsa for 40 quid and cashback if you needed it, and if you haven't witnessed Kevin Bridges tell the story of the 40 Quid Man, you're missing out.

Adding to an already peculiar morning, she announced we were going out and that the destination was to remain a surprise.

My eyes shot open and my squint-eye straightened for a brief minute. A mother–daughter outing that wasn't just her dropping me off on her way to do whatever amazing things children think adults do without them seemed like a promise of Dundee Disneyland.

Without a word, nostrils still flared and eyes still open like I'd taken speed, I went to my room and started packing a little day-trip bag. I didn't have much information on where we were going, so I just packed some essentials like my Spice Girls book and poster, a yo-yo I'd acquired in a fair playtime bet, and my knee pads that would one day prove useful counterparts to the skateboard my mum had promised me. I took the bag through and stared at her, in what was probably a really creepy way. I described the bag's contents, and she explained I wouldn't need any of it and told me to go and brush my teeth.

I knew it. We were going on holiday. 'Far out, Big Max. You are forgiven for the last 12 years!'

We were, in fact, not going on holiday.

We were going to the dentist.

Worse still, we were going to the dentist in order to be told I needed braces.

When I sobbed about the social suicide she was forcing me into and asked her, 'Why, oh dear God, why?', she said because I was the child and she was the adult.

Finally, after about three weeks of constant tears and threats of suicide by jumping off the three-foot wall at the back of our flat, she caved and said I didn't have to get them, but also informed me I would regret it when I was older.

She was right.

Regret is real.

Plus, Invisalign aren't that invisible, but they do work and now you can't see any of my teeth when my mouth is closed.

On the downside, I can't open beer bottles with them anymore.

Don't you dare ...

Ole Snaggletooth threw my things out. Again.

Any child psychologist worth their salt could tell you that's a sure way to raise a hoarder.

I got in from school, kicked off my shoes and, while looking down, noticed the empty space that had until that morning been used as a resting place for all the books I was copying from. (And yet still I was receiving mediocre scores in class. It's a real conundrum.)

I dominantly waltzed into the living room, rounding the door to look Scotland's own Hitler in the face. I was like, 'Bitch, where are all my things and how are you not old enough for a home yet?' But more, 'Mum, have you moved my stuff from the hall, please, thank you, love you, sorry if this seems unreasonable! Please, and thanks again.'

She didn't even look away from the TV – not even a momentary glance in my direction. So I proceeded to call her a monster – a befitting name for the attitude. But not like the other times, when I said it in my head. This time I said it out loud. Vocally. Within earshot of the book-throwing monster herself.

In my defence, do you know how long it took to find things to plagiarise back then? The Internet wasn't quite the same magical place as it is today, so it was much, much harder!

'Don't you dare call me that!'

Clearly, the most bothersome part of the situation had been pinpointed. She did not agree that she was, you know ... a bit of a c*nt. She thrust herself off the couch and in my direction.

Oh boy. The devil had been summoned.

All I had to do to escape being beaten like a piñata was to open the living-room door; cross the hall in one bounding jump; open and run out of the front door; go down the stone steps three at a time, four if manageable, out into the winter evening; cross a busy main road in a city of 150,000 people; and land safely at my gran's house ... 12 miles away.

Like most brains undergoing trauma, mine began putting everything into slow motion, so I had a lead of about 0.2 seconds to lunge for the yank-operated handle of the living-room door that, by all accounts, was the first hurdle in my long run to freedom.

That is, other than the more problematic hurdle of my legs staying exactly where they were while my mind imagined they were moving.

It wasn't until after that learning curve that she let me know the papers and books were under her bed and that if I wanted them, all I needed to do was ask.

A compelling idea never before tried ... except for two actual minutes before she suggested it!

Guiding tip: Never underestimate how adroitly the trap for you is set.

I am not a monster – Myra Hindley is a monster! Do you want me to go and get her?

There was a lot of monster talk around me, clearly. Not really the kind that most kids hear about – beasts lurking under your bed waiting to snatch at your ankles after dark – but the kind of monster that looks like Ian Huntley or Jeffrey Dahmer.

I had one job, and it was to not get on my mum's tits. As is overwhelmingly apparent, I got on my mum's tits.

There was a day in the summer holidays, sometime in the early 2000s, when I told her I'd iron her clothes for her, because I'm nice like that.

No, I didn't burn them, calm down – that's far too predictable!

God, you should all expect more from me than that. Come on, guys. Get your sh*t together.

Okay, I burned them.

The iron was up too high and they did get a little singed in areas, but there was no burn mark, so let's all settle down.

Instead, I got brown polish on her white linen trousers, and it was what anyone with a good sense of humour would call 'perfectly placed'.

It's a mistake anyone in the house could have made, because we ironed on a towel on the floor in the living room. There were many reasons for this, but the main one was that we didn't own an ironing board.

The floor-ironing spot was also often the spot where we polished our shoes. As I sat on my knees ironing the trousers, blowing the bits that were getting hard from the hot iron and dabbing the bits that were getting wet from the leaking water, I noticed the hideous brown smudge. It was smelted on the back and it was not coming off.

I remained confident that if she got them on without noticing, the day would go smoothly.

It seemed pretty reasonable to assume that we would get to wherever we were going and someone or something else would take the blame for the stain that resembled a small pebble of shite right over her arsehole.

And that might have worked if I hadn't stared at it like a four-foot idiot as we walked down the street.

She, taking her cue from me, started to search the back of her body, and, in the end, she found the nefarious stain detailing all of my shortcomings as both ironer and liar.

What else could I do? I had to come clean, so I was like, 'Look, Mum, you shit yourself!' But really, *really* loudly.

She looked as though I was about to sh*t myself.

In a bid to deflect all attention, I began saying, 'I think my mum shit herself!' to passers-by. A few of them seemed moderately interested in the full-grown woman who'd just took a hot one on the street corner. Some more than others.

Alchy Kev still calls her 'Shitty Breeks' when he sees her, and it's always touching to see.

She reacted like she was Anna fucking Wintour, though. You'd have thought an artist had cut the trousers.

Relax, Big Max, they were from Primark, not Prada, doll.

She marched me back to the house and, among some other hurtful names, called me a monster!

Well, I never! In all my days I have never been called something so inappropriate and heinous, and that's including at school, where the boys were still calling me Manzie Kennels. So I shouted back, 'No, you're a monster!', to which she replied with the edge of her voice, 'No, Myra Hindley is a monster! Do you want me to go and get her?'

DING, DING, DING! – the sound of round two.

Let's just take a step back here and analyse this situation:

1. Who started the name-throwing game we'd found ourselves in? Her, she did.

2. Who called who a 'monster' to begin with for slightly altering the colour on one small patch of a pair of eight-pound trousers? She did, I do believe.

3. Who then was she likening me to? One half of the Moors murderers.

Most of that, I could forgive. But when she used Myra and my paralysing fear of her against me for shits and giggles, she really got my goat.

Although she used to majorly own me with threats of Myra from a zero-distance range, this time seemed different – she didn't chuckle after and tell me she was joking 'for now'.

Obviously, I was shit scared of Myra, mainly because only a crazy psychopath wouldn't be.

As a quick tangent, is it not hard to believe no one could tell just by looking at her? Like, it wasn't a dead giveaway she was a child murderer? What about the fact she actually looked like the Child Catcher with MAC foundation on? No one saw it coming … really? Wow, Britain, you really need to get your shit together.

Again, Savile? No one? Seems odd.

Who am I to judge, though? I really fancy all ginger men. We all have our burdens to bear.

Anyway, Big Max had just threatened me with breaking a known child murderer out of jail and letting her babysit, so I felt we couldn't get any lower.

I miscalculated.

Not *that* long after this, she told me that Myra had escaped from prison and watched me crumble like a day-old biscuit.

I don't know about you guys, but it seems clear to me that she was a terrible person. But also hilarious in a really sick way, because she'd have really mauled you if you'd breathed on me too hard.

Guiding tip: Never underestimate how low a parent will stoop to stop you from being a dickhead.

Starting a fight with your parents (or boyfriend/girlfriend/S.O.) is a great way to get out of doing something you really don't want to do…

Lay the groundwork in advance so it's not obvious.

Call me 'Auntie Max' when we get in here

Have all of you noticed that all of our parents think we are prettier than nearly everyone else?

The sad truth is that we can't all be above average (and better looking than our cousins and mates) and not all humans are good-looking, so there are literally children everywhere who have faces only their own mothers love.

I know, I should've warned you before letting you read that. It's a bummer, isn't it?

However, there's not a mum on the planet that wears thicker mum-goggles than mine! They are like milk bottles, but doubled up.

My first word was 'Si' ... so she told everyone I was already bilingual.

I made a cow noise when I was nine months old, so she told the whole family I was going to be a vet or Ace Ventura.

One time, I accidentally got an answer about some art piece right when we were watching *Who Wants to Be a Millionaire?* and so she thought I was going to be an expert.

The list goes on.

The real burden is that I probably peaked in about 1993; people still thought I was cute. I didn't know enough actual words to talk enough so that people could find out I was probably the dumbest person they knew, but I was also no longer sh*tting myself. So, all positives really.

Big Max, though, she loved my face even though the rest of the family called me 'Rubber lips'. The crooked eye thing wasn't that noticeable. It was like one eye was looking at your face while the other was looking at your armpit, and I look about a lot when I speak, so it's hard to catch.

In saying all this, she herself was not too shabby to look at when she was a young 20-something broad out in the big city, and we all hoped I'd look more like her the older I got and less like an ugly bastard. I'm only 30, so there's time.

When we were younger, it used to be next-next level embarrassing walking past a building site and hearing the workmen wolf-whistle at her.

Obviously, I was unaware that when I was older, I'd be mapping out sites around the city and *casually* walking by to fill the old self-esteem tank up when times were hard.

Now, alas, she kind of has more chins than the Chinese phonebook, but I'd be really mad if anyone else said that about her.

She says she has SAD (Seasonal Affective Disorder), and her yearly weight gain is a by-product of it, but I think she has FBS (Fat Bastard Syndrome), and, sadly, the older you get, the less you care about more and more.

But back to the point in hand: she was a looker and she felt our chances of getting things for free were diminished when people knew we were closely related. She, young Big Max, felt her good looks were better served when she could pretend she was an aunt and not a mother. So, if we were going somewhere a male might be serving us, like the post office, the bus, the shops, the shopping centre, the taxi rank, any restaurant, the dentist, the doctor's, the takeaway shop, the coffee shop, the 'Housing', or any public place in general, I was to call her Auntie Max, and I did it gladly.

It wasn't a favour. I wasn't all that eager for people to know she was my mum. Eventually, it backfired on poor Aunt Max, and harder than Uncle Buck's car.

I finally clicked on to the fact that the advantage in this charade was mine. Things like, 'Well, *Auntie Max*, you must remember that my *mum* told us I am allowed to wear my cardigan like a turban' were mine to spout freely when we were someplace I did not want to be and she was taking a long-ass time.

A perfectly good stranger observing the situation could have been forgiven for mistaking her grimace for a sweet aunt's smile. The price I'd later pay would always be worth it.

And also screaming 'You're not my mummy' in public places was another fav, especially when she was dragging me and it looked like I was being kidnapped.

Guiding tip: Just as in all other areas of life, the small wins are fundamental in shaping the big ones. Take them when and where possible.

Scottish kids:

How do we apply for university or study abroad?

Scottish schools:

Shut the f**k up and do the ceilidh.

You'll be pretty when you grow up and you're beautiful to me!

'All the Reynolds go through a funny phase!'

What she meant by 'funny' was that we all look like Honey Boo Boo for a few years in our early youth and about a decade after that, too. Each of us, from age 7 to 17, could've made the entire cast of *Sesame Street* cry, and I, in particular, had a nose that only the Jewish community could love. I grew into it and can no longer smoke a cigar in the shower.

Her mum-goggles remained, of course, but even they seemed to be losing strength around my early teens.

One time in particular, though, I was hit pretty hard – metaphorically speaking, for once.

Somehow, I was taken in by the popular girls at school. It was the group the rest of the school, for the most part, thought was filled with hot girls. Like an American-movie type of situation, but with worse teeth.

However, no matter what lies I may have told myself at the time, no one actually thought I was popular.

Apart from me. Obviously.

Let's just clarify the 'taken in' part first. When I got to high school, I wasn't one of those kids who were naturally popular and able to produce a feeling of unworthiness in the other kids just because they existed. For the love of all that's good, that was not me.

My inner geek and I were in a constant battle. Dork-me thought the bright lights shining down illuminating the computers with a godly glow in classroom 4W, the sexiest classroom in school, were calling me and my binary soul to them.

The superuser of my body, 14-year-old me, the one who was desperate to be popular, was more about padding her bras with toilet roll for extra bounce and gelling down the leg hair my mum had forbidden me from shaving.

My social status was also not elevated given the fact I looked like a golf club from the side, but Raquel let me hang around with her. Raquel was a good egg. She saw the best in everyone, and her dad always fed you when you went to his house – what was not to like?

But we hung around with a gaggle of wenches so wild and monstrous in nature that frankly I am shocked some of them aren't wreaking havoc in Cornton Vale. They got up to all kinds of ridiculous shit that was both educational and terrifying.

One by one, picture, if you will, each of the gaggle I was now thrilled to be a part of. We'll start with Barbara.

Barbara once shaved a man's eyebrows off with the help of her older brother when their mum had a party and was too high on cocaine to notice what her kids were scalping, which only serves as a reminder that it wasn't poor Barbara's fault she was a bit of a bitch. Barbs was kind of a barbarian from day one, but she was popular because she was cute to look at.

Carla was actively trying to sleep with her best friend's dad ... or brother, she wasn't fussed, just as long as it was one of them.

Macie was sleeping with her boyfriend's cousin, while her best friend, Fiona, had started shoplifting and selling pretty good Topshop products to the years above in return for their bursary money.

One girl, Brogan, wasn't any trouble, but she couldn't be taught that men don't have functioning nipples, and her boyfriend had also started selling us some soft-core drugs.

One of us, Clara, was ditching school to hang out with a married man, but we all embraced that love because he'd buy her alcohol and she'd share it with us on the weekends (when he was with his kids). It worked out well for everyone.

Another would become obsessed with Barbara's brother and would eventually start cutting classes to hang with him – that would be me.

I should point out here that I'm not getting our school mixed up with *Teen Narcos*. We were much more savage to one another, and I've never seen anyone bang someone else's dad on *Narcos*.

So now to the point: Barbara, before most of the above had ever occurred, was forced to give me an invitation to her 13th birthday party, which was in a pub in the city centre. I asked my mum if I could go and immediately she said no, so naturally I cried like everyone I'd ever known had just been murdered.

Big Max eventually asked 'what in the hell the problem' was, and I let her know that I wasn't popular; I was the only girl wearing pigtails to school because I hadn't yet worked out how to iron the back of my hair, and I was for sure being called Manzie Kennels more often than 'Casper' – my old, more preferable nickname.

Unbelievably, she retracted her earlier statement and read me her new decision: 'You can go, but I'm dropping you off and picking you up. You can go from 7 to 9 p.m.'

Me: 'But the party starts at 8.30 p.m.'

Her: 'I know you heard what I *just* said!'

I really should have known something was coming...

Forward to the night of the party, and I was feeling pretty good. I had applied my make-up in a reasonable fashion: I looked a lot like a goth's dream, even though that was definitely not what I was going for, but my mum had ensured my face was the same colour as my neck: peanut butter coloured. My fav. I would recommend Superdrug's 2002 £1 foundation for sure.

I was readily equipped with six-inch platform shoes (don't mistake these for platform heels; they were raised six inches from heel to toe).

I walked in. There was no music. People looked at me like I came in strangling a puppy and then went on pretending to ignore me from behind stray glances.

I clocked Raquel and tried to wave at her, but my arms were feeling a bit heavy after sitting in the car hyperventilating and begging my mum and stepdad to 'Just take me home!' while fanning my nerve rash from my neck and chest with the lid of their pizza box.

I promptly sat by Raquel, who probably wanted the ground to swallow her up immediately, but she didn't say it because she's not a prick.

I stayed for one drink – a soda – and then my half hour was up. I went home and slept soundly knowing that on Monday morning I would be fully accepted into the UK's most vicious gang – a gaggle of 13-year-olds that could've made the guys in *Sons of Anarchy* look like society's dream.

No one thought that was going to pan out, did they …

First period on Monday was a sore one. When it was intimated the invitation was given to me more out of sheer pity and less out of *actually* requesting my presence, it was a bit of a Debbie Downer.

It was also gently delivered to me at the same time that I wasn't exactly cool enough to be there (I know, it could bring a tear to a glass eye). So, like the young fledgling I was, I cried on the inside like a real winner. Then I went home that night and burst into fits of tears that might have seemed a tad overdramatic to anyone not a teenager. My psychotic breakdown had commenced.

I told my mum about it, and instead of her usual urge to beat the perpetrators of my sadness down, she instead said softly, enveloping me in a tight hug, 'You'll be cool and pretty when you're older, Max!'

Comforting? Mmmm, not really. I just took the opportunity to wipe some of my snotters on her dressing gown.

'And you're beautiful to me,' she added, as she always did, which also didn't make me feel any better at all.

Note that most of us were lovely in our own ways and we weren't bad. I mean, there are children who ask for pineapple on pizza, so we weren't heinous, but *man alive* were we mean to one another.

School for me was like one really long stint in a psych ward where I wanted to be the most popular patient. *PSYCH!!!*

(See what I did there.)

Big Max always said that it was good that I wasn't pretty at school because it meant I would develop a personality, but I don't think that worked out the way she planned, because my personality through school was akin to Kim Jong-un's as far as she was concerned.

I reckon I'm a super late bloomer though. By the time I hit 35, I bet I'm peaking. Or fat.

Guiding tip: Don't do your eyebrows, and ignore boys until around age 20. Being popular is a massive hassle.

I know you're lying to me!

The deceitful wench used sorcery that Voldemort himself couldn't conjure. We'd reached a point where she was able to tell every lie in quasi-time.

Reading the diary detailing my most private, vulnerable and 'rent-hating thoughts was now beneath her.

She was leading the advanced class. 'The Eye of the Tiger' played everywhere she dared to walk.

You know Bette Midler? You know when she played Winifred in the movie *Hocus Pocus* and looked at her sister as if she had a surprise arsehole on her face? That was the exact (!!!) face my mum used to pull when she was about to verbally drop-kick me via a glib comment.

With a precursory look (see Winifred below) and then five short words, she made me believe she'd developed the miraculous ability to read my rampantly fabricating mind.

'I know you are lying!' she'd smirk with one raised eyebrow.

HOWWWWWW, though? I'd howl internally. *How do'th the soothsayer know? What powers must she have?*

I was sure there was a God and that he absolutely hated me.

Turns out, bitch didn't know shiiiii'! She was, however, a world-class bender of the truth herself – a mind athlete.

She was studying at college, as was my stepdad, and between them, they had learned that they could use their studies to outsmart the only idiot under 16 in the house.

She told me – and he, now the chief accomplice to my teenage pain, nodded in agreement – that when a person lied, their eyes always went up and to the right.

Informational gold.

SWISH! Bring on the eye contact!

I wouldn't have to shout my lies from behind the kitchen door a day longer!

Science!

Yes!

I had about 1,800 lies saved and ready to be pulled right out whenever the mood struck, and now I had the world's best cheat sheet. It had been handed straight from one person's fuckery-pouch and placed straight into my own!

I put it straight in the mind-bank and began basking in the glory of this newly acquired information that could propel me forward like a rebellious, flying, unstoppable idiot.

Suddenly Lie-Hound Reynolds was conquerable. My Magneto–Shaw moment had finally arrived, and the mayhem I planned was second to none.

All I had to do to accomplish my new, very achievable dream of lying and getting away with it was to look up and to the left.

 EEA-ZEE! Nothing to it. Up and to the left. I treated my right-hand side's peripheral vision like I was blind there for weeks!

She'd say things like, 'Did you clean your room?' A nod from me, followed by an UP AND TO THE LEFT glance.

'Have you taken money from my purse?' Shocked face, followed by an UP AND TO THE LEFT glance.

'Have you been going to school?' Universal 'obviously!' teen-face, followed by, yup, you got it: an UP AND TO THE LEFT glance.

'Are you lying to me?' [Insert witty remark here, plus a young, now nearly cross-eyed me, looking up and far to the left.]

'Did you take the rubbish down to the bin or throw it out of the window again?' Disappointed shake of the head, followed by a soft, wistful glance up and to the left, and a complementary 'Mum, Ma, Maxine, Max, come on. Would I lie to you?'

Ahhh, sweet success! I concluded that my guileful tactics had led me straight into adulthood. I'm not too sure how I came to that understanding, but, nonetheless, I was pretty steadfast in my belief.

Yep, I was that easy to trick. Turns out your eyes will automatically go in that direction when you're constructing something imagined ... In other words, when you're pulling a Bill Clinton and being a Bob Cryer.

My guardians had, in stealth mode, metaphorically slammed me by misrepresenting science to a degree that should be punishable. Big Max gently walked me to the edge of the proverbial cliff and waited for me to jump off like a grade-A moron, killing my freedom dead.

Smite me, oh savage smiter!

1 – 0 Big Max; well played, my good woman, well played.

Eventually, she told me the truth and proceeded to rattle off each of the lies I'd thrown out in that past fortnight. By the end of it, she'd nearly lost her voice and I owed her three weeks' manual labour and a lot of stolen change.

Guiding tip: Petition for better science in schools. Sue your old school for not teaching you a useful thing in six whole goddamn years.

An accurate portrait of me lying, thinking I was getting away with it. Sad moments.

Drinking is bad for you

One time, we – the gaggle of populars and me – decided we'd worked hard enough at school that week, and we were going to skip class. Wednesdays were becoming very Monday-ish for us all.

We went to our usual rendezvous point (the community shops on Alpine Road) and waited on a man – a man we'll name Bill, who was the lunchtime drunkard – to fall out of the classy betting establishment situated just steps from our Catholic school.

When that moving poetry fell out of the bookies, we knew we had but a few moments to bribe him with £2, most likely stolen in 20p's from our parents, into buying us four litres of cider.

God bless the bejesus out of Bill.

Not an hour later, though, I had hard cider come straight out of my nose when, out of the corner of my rotating eye, I caught sight of my mum walking towards us behind said shops.

I had visions of her chasing me at full pelt for a mile – like a lion after a gazelle – to the nearest police station, where I would take cover. But something so spectacular then happened that I was, for a moment, sure I was so disastrously drunk I must be comatose and dreaming: she walked right past me.

She just sauntered merrily on, talking on the phone to someone clearly so important she'd been unable to identify her own daughter in a crowd of drunken teens. I was both relieved and outraged.

She was slipping, and, clearly, I was going to end up an alcoholic or in social services, because she'd given too much at the start of my life and was floundering as a parent in the middle.

When I got home the next day, after staying the night with my aunt, who wouldn't have noticed I was drunk if I'd pumped my own stomach in front of her, I cautiously raised the subject of alcohol by telling her that I was taking part in a project at school.

I reckoned that if she had seen me but had chosen to walk by, then that had to be because she was waiting for the time to strike, in which case I'd be skinned alive and buried in the back garden quicker than Bill took our two-pound bribe. But all she said on the matter was that drinking was bad for you and she was glad she hadn't had to beat me for it – yet.

Then she gave me a warm smile that made me feel guilty ... guilty for not finishing my half-litre of cider the day before. I was raging!

The 'yet': then I did get drunk, and she did catch me.

I was at a party with the rest of my schoolmates where the theme of the night seemed to be asking me if 'Albert's meat was from the butcher's', even though I hadn't slept with him ... but when have teenagers ever let facts get in the way of a good story?

I myself had helped in perpetuating the rumour that someone's dad had a secret child with the mum of another of our friends. We were wrong, but, still, we spread it far and wide.

Before I could set the record straight, Barbara's mum cast me out onto the streets because I pushed all 200lbs of her out of the way so I could proceed to – politely – spew in her bathroom and not in her hallway. She kicked me out of her house so fast I was unable to comprehend the curiosity of the situation – the fact she was awake and not snacking.

I got halfway down the street when I heard the forever-pleasing sound of police sirens. I looked behind me to see I was being followed by no fewer than four police cars. In actual fact, it was just one police car and a lot of cider, which my body was about to vomcano out of my mouth and nose at the same time.

I know I was harsh on the obese woman who let a gaggle of rowdy, underage teens party in her house all night after buying them alcohol and then kicked at least one of them (me) out, but she was no match for the Man-Grinch that greeted me outside of St. Peter and Paul's Primary School in the Hilltown area of the city, so brace yourselves.

He had me on my tummy in pretzel before I could make out that she was, in fact, female. Then I puked on her shoes, which looking back were a bit large for the average-sized woman's foot.

She unceremoniously threw me in the back of the car – cuffed, no less – smashing her man-knee into my back like it was made of stone and pushing the weight of Shamu onto me. And then she told me that I was a 'ginger little c*nt' who was 'in a lot of trouble'.

She was indeed correct on all counts.

That's not an ideal way to introduce yourself to a drunk teen, though. Alas, she was doomed to the fiery depths of teenage sentiment and I gave her unbridled abuse for the next four hours.

When we arrived at the station, they put me in a room that I'm going to have to make up the details about because, honestly, I can't remember a thing about it. For the sake of storytelling, picture your own version of a police interrogation room, but then imagine the drunkest person on the planet pinballing around it. Thanks.

A point came, as it does in every young girl's life, when I found myself asking: is my mum becoming more annoying, or am I becoming more angry?

It was her.

I do, however, remember what cracked her: she'd vetoed me going to the bathroom to continue my spewathon, and so I was again forced to do it on her shoes. She laughed at me, and, to be fair, it was laughable; I was complaining I had flu-ingles, which I'd self-diagnosed. Flu times shingles. A real disease. Don't look it up though.

In the eternity it took for my mum to come and collect me, she-devil made me clean the newly aired cider up with toilet roll. Now is a great time to note that Dundee's Bell Street station isn't springing for Andrex, and I cleaned a lot of it up with my own hand. And she told me she was getting social services in to take me from my mum.

Now, I wasn't Big Max's biggest fan. Frankly, she was starting to wear me out, but she was my only mum and constant defender, so I was forced to go on a rampage. I told she-devil gently that she was 'a fucking monster' and 'let the lord baby Jesus, the Allfather and the Dick Gods never afford a teenager' to her, the 'butcher's-daughter-looking-ass creature'.

That done it.

She started to weep and walked out while her partner smirked and gave me a Mars bar, which tasted delicious, even in the aftermath of a spew session registering about a nine on the spewer scale.

I just want to say that I'm usually a delight drunk, and, looking back, it does seem a bit harsh to have said all that to someone who'd given me a lift a bit closer to where I actually lived. However, I'd also like to point out that the Mars bar more or less seems to prove that she was a bitch ... unless that man was also a monster.

Cue getting reamed: my mum collected me from the police station and walked me home the short distance to our house on Princes Street.

But it turned out not to be that short given I was one-stepping forward and two-stepping back the duration.

She laughed a lot, but I think that's only because she thought I wouldn't remember in the morning.

She was half right, because the following morning I struggled to remember there was a thing called laughter at all. I needed sunglasses to open up the fridge, and the light in it was broken.

That day, an ineffable amount of viciousness was bestowed upon me. She and my stepdad took me round the entire family to tell them about my cider-and-blackcurrant binge, and the pair of bastards let family members sneak up on me from behind and make loud noises so close to me it felt like they were inside my head.

They let them mock-puke in re-enactments, and I believe pictures were taken, too. As well as all that, they let them wave beers under my nose in an effort to see if I'd puke more.

I cried on the inside like a real winner, as always. Then cried for real when I got home, as always.

I also got grounded for a month, but I was an outright champion in school for at least a full week after, so it was kind of win–win for me. I was treated like a legend by my peers but didn't have the pressure of outdoing my drunk self for a month, because my mum was using our house as a corrections facility for her sole (and soul) prisoner.

No ... Because I said so, that's why! (Sometimes said as 'Can you buggery!')

I don't believe I'm exaggerating when I say that it took at least three business days to ask my mum anything, and a further two business days to get an answer if it wasn't just a straight-out 'No!'

I will, however, concede that Big Max came through for me a few of these times by denying me my questionable desires.

Obviously, being a natural oppressor, she didn't just deny requests and have no more to say on any given matter, but if it wasn't for her, I would currently be the proud owner of a few facial tattoos, a couple of henna tattoos and, according to one friend with said henna tattoo, Hepatitis C. I'd also have sported a skinhead, dreads and a pierced nose, tummy, eyebrow, bridge, lip, neck, nail and collarbone; and, at one point, I would've had black hair and gold caps. I'd also have changed my name to Trinity.

However, on other occasions, she was unnecessarily unfair.

'Mum, can I stay at (any friend's) house tonight?'
    'No.'

'Mum, can we move to Australia?'
    'No.'
    'Why?'
    'Because!'

'Mum, can we move into Adam's car so we don't have to give the dog away?'
    'No.'

'Mum, can I watch *The Exorcist*?'
    'No.'

'Mum, can I get one of these tattoos everyone is getting at school? They disappear after five years?'
    'No.'

'Why do you hate me?'
'Come over here and I'll give you a scar!'
'No, thank you.'

'Mum ...'
'No!'
'You don't even know what it is!'
'You took too long, so no.'

'Mum, can I go to school in America?'
'Shut up. No.'

'Mum ... You know what, it doesn't matter, because you'll just say no anyway!'
'I might not!'
'Well, can I ...'
'No.'

'Mum, can we go and live in Australia?'
'Again, no.'
'Why not? Is it because you hate me?'
'No, it's because Gran doesn't get free international calls.'
'We wouldn't take her?'
'No.'

'Mum, can I run the Tay Bridge at night after school?'
'I don't know, Max. Ask me again later.'
Roughly three long days later ...

'Mum, can I run the Tay Bridge in the evening after school?'

'No.'

I'm gonna go out on a limb here and assume the reason I wasn't allowed to run the bridge we lived about a millimetre on the map from was because she thought she would have to run it with me. And as we've already discussed, the bitch was lazy.

No! That's not right!

You can't keep a child locked indoors all day, every day, and we didn't have a garden at our house, so, eventually, when I began to be allowed to explore the world off of the landing in our tenement in Ardler, Big Max went into overdrive with the rules.

She started out by saying she only had a few rules: no running, no falling, no loitering, no swearing, no shouting, no mischief, no drugs, no getting dirty, no sickness, no standing too near to other children and especially no talking to strangers.

Big Max: 'What do you do if a man comes up to you and says he has puppies for you to pet?'

Me: 'Ask him to bring them to me to pet?'

Big Max: 'No! That's not right!'

Big Max: 'What do you do if a man comes up to you and says he'll buy you sweeties if you get in his car?'

>Me: 'Ask him to just bring them to me?'
>Big Max: 'No! That's not right!'

Big Max: 'What do you do if a man stops in his car and asks you to get in and show him where something is?'

>Me: 'Step back from the window, point him to Asda and then run!'
>Big Max: *Gets mum-goggles out* 'Yes! Oh my god, my child is a genius!'

Big Max: 'What do you do if a woman comes up to you and offers you to pet her puppies?'

>Me: 'See if she looks like Myra Hindley?'
>Big Max: 'No, that's not right!'

I'll make you one – the one with the Provy man

We couldn't always afford all of the things we wanted. She usually wanted electricity, hot water, food and rent money. I usually wanted a desk with a drawer attached and whatever my friends were getting.

I had a desk, but no drawer. My desk's top had recently been vacated by my portable TV thanks to the Provy man, Ken, shouting through the letterbox that he knew we were in because he could see the light from the TV flickering off the walls. At first we'd attempted to solve this sad problem by putting a large piece of cardboard over the small window at the top of my bedroom door, but, alas, it wasn't enough, and one night Ken shouted through to let us know that we 'weren't fooling anyone', so my mum made the executive decision to pay the debt back.

Just kidding. We threw the TV into the junk cupboard, only to be brought out on special occasions, like if Ken, the Provy man, died.

I always liked Ken. He used to see me playing on the stairs of our landing and ask, 'Is your mum home?'

I would invariably say, 'Yeah, but she told me to tell you no.' And he would always say, 'Well, then that's what we'll say you said', and give me 50p.

After the TV was put out of use, and I'd continued to bleat on about my need for a drawer under my desk, she finally agreed to make me one. It was constructed from a cardboard box with one short side cut off, and it was held to the underneath of the desk with duct tape and then some more duct tape.

She did warn me to begin with that it was more of a *for show* drawer, and less of a functioning one. So I wasn't that surprised when I walked into my bedroom one day and saw that the drawer had fallen to its death, and since neither of us had been the recipient of new shoes by then, she was unable to replace it.

Soon after the drawer's untimely fall came a time when I wanted Barbie furniture. My Barbie and Ken didn't have a bed to bang on (shut up, we've all done it!), and that wasn't good enough for Trinity and her shimmering PVDC synthetic hair and disproportionate and – may I say – unrealistic body. My mum built me a bed for her out of that same cardboard box.

It seemed unlikely it was going to take the weight of Ken pounding Barbie, but it held up for a while. She even made me covers for the bed out of old fabric, which she sewed with lace. That was a glorious year for the interior of my Barbie mansion. Finally, my Barbie's porn den looked worthy of the things happening in it.

Whenever it could be made, she made it. Everything from Halloween costumes to making a 'shower' in our bathroom by piercing the bottom of a litre bottle of coke and pushing it onto the end of the tap.

The biggest issue with her DIY projects was the length of time it took her to complete them. If I needed a costume for Halloween, I had to put in my request six to seven working months in advance. So, if she said she'd make you one, you knew she meant at some point in life. And that's what children need: to be taught to wait.

The dumbest thing we all believed when we were little was that adults are rich.

Can I borrow your pocket money?

Part one: How I made my fortune

I had saved up £68. In nine-year-old terms, I was a child millionaire. I got £5 every week from my gran and grandad, which I saved religiously – I held the title of 'the family Jew' for about twelve years.

I kept the cash in a drawer in their house, because, as my gran and I discussed, if I took the money home to count every hour on the hour to see if interest had hit it yet, it would be frivolously spent while I slept, or, if Big Max's mood provided the right atmosphere, as I watched and cried.

I also got £1 per week from my aunt Linn, which I also kept at her house so that my mum didn't spend it. Out of the £68, I planned to buy a pack of bouncy balls, a Furby and a mansion.

I had one hurdle to cross: not bragging.

Part two: How I lost my fortune

I began to brag.

I was willing to lose one good pound and the feeling in my ass cheeks, so I went on trying to heat a £1 coin up so that my mum would find it and it would burn her hand as she picked it up, but, alas, when she found the coin, it was cold and harmless – much to my dismay. She threw it into her purse without a second thought. I was obviously distraught.

Not too long after, camouflaged tragedy had struck and I'd told her about my £67 fortune.

She was suddenly saccharine, stroking my head instead of clattering her hand off of the back of it when I walked past her and calling me pet names like 'Marrie'.

One day she worked up the courage to ask me for a loan. I said I would, of course, loan her the money given all she did for me, but I wanted it back with interest because I'd finally worked out that my money wasn't going to gain interest automatically. Well, aside from my mum's *interest*, but hers was a different and more devilish kind of interest than banks offer.

She happily agreed to the terms knowing I was a moron.

Part three: The final demise

In our house, a bar of soap wasn't solely placed for you to wash your hands or face. It was used to facilitate punishments.

Big Max took to hiding coins under the seemingly innocent bars of Imperial Leather.

If I just wet the top of the bar, the coin wouldn't be wet, and she would know if I had or – as was the case more often than not – hadn't washed my face for school.

To get around her after she gave the jig up too early regarding the stone-dry coin, I'd started checking under the soap in the mornings and wetting the coins, because it was near to impossible to keep the soap out of my eyes, and I had a dried-up Sensitive Skin baby wipe that I was rewetting. But, finally, after my face was becoming more Nutella shaded and less pasty, she noticed that the dirt on it didn't change day-to-day and that it was probably a build-up.

I was warned: 'Max! If I find out you haven't washed your face tomorrow, you just wait and see what happens!'

I did not wash my face that tomorrow. She found out. I did not need to wait for long to see what happened.

Impeccably bad timing coupled with a bad mood that a puppy couldn't fix left me bereft of all of my happiness and fortune.

Immediately upon hearing the following words, I fell to the floor in foetal, and after a few cries and shakes, I slid along the carpet in an army crawl that I hoped wasn't startlingly noticeable, and made my way – now in stealth mode – to the house phone, from which I planned to call my grandmother while sobbing and recounting the tyrannical ways of her daughter.

Just before the last part of my body – my six-inch-long calves – passed the living-room door's threshold, I felt the claw!

The claw was Big Max's right hand, and it was always curved and ready to partake in the action. It clasped my now flailing leg and pulled me back into the living room. My underdeveloped arms quickly let go of each side of the door frame like it'd been oiled. She then hoisted me a few feet into the air and spun me around until I was on my butt, wondering how the fuck I'd let myself down so outrageously. She made me sit there while she talked about how it was a good lesson for me.

This is something I've still not forgiven her for and something I don't know if I'm emotionally capable of forgiving her for. My fortune ceased. The Bank of Big Max seemed to profit wholly, and I don't even think I got so much as a 10p Chomp out of it.

As our Queen once said, 'Bitch better have my money!'

You know I will never love another person on this planet as much as I love you!

Big Max: 'Who do you love most in the whole world?'
    Me: 'Tara [my auntie's dog] and Gran.'
    Looks at Mum
    '... And you.'

Mum: 'I love you more than I love anyone else!'
    Me: 'How much?'
    Mum: 'From here to the moon and back.'
    Me: 'You know the sun is further from us than the moon, right?'
    Mum: 'Okay, well to the sun and back!'
    Me: 'And you know that your love would be burned and evaporated before it could make its way back, right?'

Mum: 'I will never love another person on this planet as much as I love you, but be quiet.'

Part Two:
You Can Always
Talk to Me About

...

Boys

I was a slow starter – well, in comparison to most
of my friends. But let's be honest here, even if I'd
been raring to go and my mum hadn't told me
from age six that you were guaranteed AIDS from
sex, my nicknames in school were Manzie Kennels,
Big Lips Wee Tits and occasionally Casper, so I'm
not saying it was all by choice, but the fact
remains – resembling a golf club from the side,
looking like I had to run to get wet in the rain and
having Big Max add garlic to everything that was
cooked in the house meant that, all in all, I was no
catch.

     Thank you for coming to my TED Talk.
Motivational speaking is a passionate hobby of
mine.

Moving on from that touching subject to this: here's how 'it' finally went down for me (no pun intended). I made a bad decision. Twice.

What should've been a well-planned marathon of exploring turned out to be a three-minute nightmare.

There was a boy who was a lot older than me and a lot cooler. Cooler as in he didn't go to school, had no job and loved a bong. Obviously, I fell deeply in love with him.

You know how humans can smell pheromones and sense things about people in milliseconds thanks to subconscious sensory inputs? That's also not what happened here. I was just really stupid.

No, but really, you know that dragonflies seemingly fake their own deaths so they don't have to mate with unwanted males? Also not what happened here, but would've been a good shout.

So, after a long three-week wait, I decided we knew everything we needed to about one another and announced I thought we should romantically bang in my friend's upstairs bedroom, minus the bed.

But there was a duvet on the floor. It's true I nearly puked in my own mouth, although 14-year-old me thought that was a reaction to the intense love that we as a steady couple of three weeks were experiencing and nothing to do with the decision itself. But looking back, it was definitely a reaction to the fact his deepest thought was probably being a banana and my deepest thought was his banana.

The whole thing was bananas.

To make matters worse, these were the days before Big Max went to college and no longer had to read my diary. I made the mistake of detailing the event in my 'private' diary, and she made an executive choice to read it.

The Privacy Nazi, it turns out, read every page and then took it to her friend's to read every page again, but out loud. So not only did she find out every damn name I jotted down when she was particularly unpleasant, but she also, of course, found out that I was no longer a virgin, and I'd made my sexual debut.

One day, not too long after the inhumane incident had occurred and the written record of it had been produced, I left my room to get my dinner. She handed me a plate, ironically laden with some very unappetising-looking fried sausages with a side of suffering, and said to me, 'So, you've had sex. Twice, no less.'

I quickly took the plate and darted to my room, where I planned to stab myself with the butter knife. She followed me, saying, 'If you're big enough to do it, you're big enough to talk about it!' To which I answered, 'I'm not big enough for either, and I hate you!'

You'd think that the farce would end there, but it didn't. Soon thereafter, she made me go to the doctor to get tested for AIDS.

That's right ... AIDS.

When the day came to collect my results, I walked into the doctor's surgery alone, quickly adopting the white man's disgrace walk: arms hanging stiffly by my sides, head down, eyes systematically surveying the room, checking for persons familiar and persons who looked like they knew my mum or stepdad.

I finally took my turn and approached the reception desk, throat-whispered my information and added that I was 'collecting my ... *results*'.

'Results for what?' She said it a bit like she was a complete d*ckhat.

I honestly toyed with the idea of saying 'Cancer'. I almost did it, but the one part of my soul that wasn't black forbade it.

'Results for ... um .... well ... (*lowers voice further*) STIs.'

'STIs?' *Raises her piercing voice exponentially.*

Face reddens and head nods to indicate she heard me correctly.

'What were you tested for?'

Face grows dark and thunderous. 'ESSS. TEEE. IYYYYZ!'

'Yes, but which ones?'

'All of them!'

'So, gonorrhoea, chlamydia ... what else?'

Not all that thankful for the push start, I began naming the rest of all of our favourite, easy-to-pronounce STIs.

On my way out, like any well-raised teen, I gave her the middle finger and ran out of the office doors ... but first I ran into a locked one.

She looked as though she was honeycombed with sheer delight. As she chortled, the top layer of her body did the Mexican wave from scalp to gunt, and I'd guess she had a victory snack only moments later.

From then on, I coded my diary. It was a particularly rudimentary sequence of digits that involved turning the letters of the alphabet into numbers and then reversing them as I wrote.

I know, my talents have gone unnoticed for years. MI5, I live in Los Angeles; I'll do just about anything for a clean slate and an RBS account with an overdraft.

You might think she tried to crack the code herself, or maybe she left me alone, let me have some privacy.

BIG LOL again. Did you just start reading this book or forget all of the other chapters?

Nope, not Big Max; she took the book detailing my most private reflections, considerations and brilliant hate-naming over to her friend's house again. Paula was the parent to a pretty bright little boy. They offered him the tidy sum of ten big ones to crack the code.

Upon trying, he told them that I was, obviously, a downright genius and that he couldn't crack the code. Big Max, being the generous soul she is, gave him £5 for trying. Then he came to me, told me he'd obviously cracked the world's dumbest encryption and said he'd keep schtum for five of my good pounds. Which he received without one ounce of resistance.

Massive props to Jay for not being a snitch. His bravery should've been rewarded more heartily.

Guiding tip: Be nice to children your parents know; you never know when they will be asked to betray you.

Finding out you're the only reason that you're completely f*cked in life is pretty harrowing and an utter shock.

–Me, a PTSD recoverer.

(Even if you're bang-smack in the middle of ruining it when you find out.)

Drugs

I actually never took drugs when I was younger. I have tried eating weed three times now, though — twice with detrimental consequences. The first time, at the ripe old age of 18, I ate brownies. I got the munchies, ate brownies to conquer the munchies, and then got so miraculously high I thought the neighbour's Labrador was a camel and told all of my mates that I had to go home (because I honestly thought they were going to kill me). When they pointed out that it was my house, I told them they could keep it and I made my way to the back door with my back pressed to the walls so they couldn't stab me in it.

The second time, I ended up in a bush outside the Oakwood apartments in Burbank, California, just over from Universal Studios, camouflaging my clothes with dried-up leaves and trying to call my mum to let her know I was sure one of my friends, high as shit himself inside, was going to kill me. And also to say I was sorry for taking drugs. Again.

By the time my two mates found me, my legs had gone numb and I was convinced I was in a partial coma.

We did buy that weed in Arizona from a transitioning transgender man whose girlfriend was pregnant and whose hormone tablets may or may not have been mixed in during the weed harvesting process, because I'll not lie — I was very, highly emotional while cocooning for the following three days.

Now, I've been in some insane situations throughout my 30-year run, but this one takes the biscuit: the third time was indeed a cracker.

I was in a place called Muskoka in Canada. A party is hosted there every year by a rich dude whose only request is that you don't take drugs.

We took drugs.

It's very beautiful and tranquil in Muskoka, bar once per year when hoards of partiers gather for an invite-only party that spans a cluster of cottages just off a Canadian lake. I'd gone with two of my friends in the hopes of having a great time, but the enemy of youth hath decided I shall not enjoy more than two days of drinking lest it kill me, so on the third day, Geneva and I were like, 'Aight, let's chill here today and drive back to the city tonight. That way we can't drink, and tomorrow we might even function like normal humans for a while.' We agreed and started enjoying our whiskey-free day with some waterskiing and swimming.

It was all going delightfully well until someone offered us chocolate. The fat bastard in me burst to life. She did not and could not care that the chocolate was riddled with weed.

This weed, it turned out, was not fucking around. Let's fast forward to two hours later, when I woke up on the dock thinking that it was drifting away from the mainland. I shadily got up and attempted to pivot my way back to the solid earth like a fat ballerina in rubber flip-flops.

I was having a few lucid moments in between, so I knew I was high, but I was so paranoid that I felt sure I couldn't tell anyone what was happening. And there were many signs still hanging in pretty much every area as far as the eye could see saying drugs were prohibited.

After finding a little area far back from the water where I could hide quietly, I began to think of ways to undo what would turn out to be irreversible in the short term. In my few rational moments, the same moments I was now sure were going to be my last on earth, I was researching ways to get un-high. Eventually, catching myself in a coherent state, I knew I needed to look this whole cycle up. I turned to the world's most reliable interconnected highway of facts. The Internet.

What a shit idea.

After a somewhat put-together Google search of 'how not to be high anymore?', I found a very informative article online that took three hours to load (but it was actually only 45 seconds), and it said you could try to exercise it off or sniff black pepper. Frantically, but also in stealth mode, I started searching for black pepper between five of the closest cottages.

I managed to find several small packets of single-serve black pepper. Coming to my senses momentarily once more, I thought to myself, *This is absolutely never, ever, ever gonna work.* Then I sniffed it like two long lines of black cocaine, and it hurt. My nostrils started to burn intensely, and then one started to bleed slightly, and my mouth started to heat up and itch, too.

It was in that moment I knew I was forever a moron.

So, just to recap, I can confirm the advice 'sniff pepper' does not work.

Having also read exercise will burn a high off quickly, I went for a jog. In a shocking plot twist, I got lost and can confirm exercise also does not work.

The further into the Canadian mountains I got, the more I was sure I was in the Balinese jungle. Having only been once before, I couldn't be sure, but the monkeys climbing the trees seemed to confirm it.

In case you hadn't realised by the mention of monkeys in Canada, my hallucinations were beginning to worsen. Sometimes all I could see was technicolour, and then sometimes I was in Bali and all was green. A deep green. Some might even say a dark weed green.

Finally, after the Internet had so devastatingly let me down for the first time in my life, something in my mind told me that nature had the cure. As I ran up some steep hills in the Canadian wilderness, I came to my senses. Stopped. Took a look around, identified the cure and proceeded to eat a common tree leaf.

My mouth was drier than the Sahara in a drought, so all the little mashed-up green fibres formed little balls of green and clung from my teeth like I was growing basil in my mouth, but the hallucinations were still prevalent, so I didn't know if the green in my teeth was real or not. But I soon found out.

After what felt like hours in the wilderness, I also knew I had to get back to the cottages even though I was fairly certain I'd been lost in the Balinese hills for three days now and everyone would be gone.

I started to make my way to where I was sure the homes that had so recently offered me shelter, asking in return only that I didn't take drugs, lay. If, that is, they hadn't drifted off into the lakes and oceans beyond, as it looked as though they would do when I made my great dancing escape.

I didn't make my way back alone, thankfully. There was one extremely surprising visitor. Even if I gave you a million-gazillion years, you'd never guess who showed up. Okay, have one guess ...

William Wallace. There's no way you guessed that. Zero points.

And he wasn't just 6ft tall. No. He was a giant, standing at a high person's estimate of 60ft.

He told me to stop eating leaves like a f*cking idiot. The cure for what had ailed me wasn't in plant. He obviously broke the news to me in pure Scots as popularised by Mel Gibson.

It's no biggie, but Thor was there, too (for when William had to chill for a bit and sharpen his blade, and, yeah, he looked exactly like Hemsworth).

After William broke the news to me that leaves weren't going to cut it and Thor laughed like he might have really been Loki, I did what any mastermind would do and filmed myself on my phone checking my teeth. A beautiful sight to behold.

I looked like Number Five from *The Umbrella Academy*, but a lot fatter. In the video, I'm saying, 'You're doing this because you're high. William said leaves won't cure you, you sniffed black pepper and you don't know what's real and what isn't. You're a total idiot ... Who said that?'

It's absolutely, frighteningly, worryingly, the best thing I've ever filmed. It's comedy gold, and it will never be witnessed by another soul.

Alas, there were a few other pit stops along the way that even the combined efforts of William and Thor couldn't protect me from. For instance, I had to make time to stand in front of a court made up of my family, friends and peers to plead on each of the sins I'd committed throughout my entire life, and I had to relive each one in full detail. It was lovely ... I really enjoyed it. There's absolutely no way I need therapy. The case where I was considering pushing my mum out of a window in our family home went really well ...

Finally, I arrived back at the cottages. I was hiding in my car when an angel who did not seem to be high at all emerged, floating towards me, smiling softly.

I finally recognised her as our friend Laura, who promised to look after me and ever so gently walked me to where Geneva was being kept, given she'd had a similar trip on what must've been some Grade-A weed.

Laura found a little back room for us to sleep it all off in. Although she had some trouble getting us to agree to sleep ... The giggles hit us both pretty badly, and I was still struggling to tell what was real and what wasn't. But when I finally woke up a few hours later ... I WAS STILL HIGH.

And that's about it in a nutshell.

To note, my uncle died of sniffing glue. Although he died before I was born, it kind of stuck with me, and my mum's words – 'You will be the one to die if you and your friends take drugs' – struck deeper than some of the rest of the bullshit she told me, like 'You aren't a ginger, you've got strawberry blonde hair', or 'You don't have a wonky eye. It's how that mirror is hanging.'

In any case, it shouldn't have come as a shock that she was, shall we say, a little *on edge* about drugs. And what I mean by that is this: I probably could have gotten her to buy me a dog if I'd told her it sniffed for drugs.

So, returning to the case with Big Max. When I got home from school from around third year onwards, she used to check my eyes for signs I was taking drugs. She also used to threaten me with drug tests. Not all heroes wear capes.

Cue the straw that broke the camel's back: after deciding we'd had enough school for one day, my friends and I retired to a *free* house for the remainder of what should've been schooling hours. And even though she puffed smoke around our house all day, so it was like we lived in a hearth, that did nothing to diminish her eyesight, and when I walked in and we locked eyes, Jesus must have spoken to her again, and my butthole has never been tighter.

Some parents ease into conversations. They sit you down, make you feel like you're in a safe environment, and then start off by saying you can talk to them, tell them anything. That was not my life.

'What drugs have you been taking? Tell me, you little shit!'

'I haven't been taking drugs,' I squeezed out through the only bit of my windpipe that she wasn't clutching with her claw.

'You'd better tell me before you pass out from them and I don't know what to tell the hospital!' she spat out frantically.

'I'm going to pass out because I can't breathe!' I said breathlessly, clutching her hand in an effort to break its grasp on my throat.

'Well, what KIND OF DRUGS ARE THOSE!'

'I can't breathe because you're choking me!' I said, feeling dizzy. My sight was starting to get patchy, and I'd already decided that if I passed out, I was walking right into that light all, 'Jesus, I've arrived. Let's talk about the prozzy. I'm intrigued.'

She finally let go, but she was still asking about the drugs I, Pablo Escobar, was hiding. I remember thinking, *Right, screw it, let's just go with the truth! She's always banging on about it, saying there'll be no ramifications if I tell it straight away.*

'I haven't been taking drugs! I went to my friend's instead of class and used her mum's eyedrops.'

I misread the situation. The truth was a terribly flawed and stupid plan. The road straight into Shitsville had shortened.

'Eyedrops? Oh really! Do you think I sailed up the Clyde on a banana boat yesterday? Think I'm zipped up the back? Well, I hope you enjoyed it, because you're moving school and you can forget your friends!'

No more eyedrops or drugs came near me for at least five years. Am I not supposed to get a badge?

Sex

Way before the diary and the stoner I let defile me at the tender age of 14, I got my birds-and-the-bees talk from my mum, which was demonstrated with a Jaffa Cake and a toothpick.

She held up a sharp toothpick in one hand, which she then pummelled through the soft side of the Jaffa Cake she was holding up in her other. She smashed it with such barbarity that the orange filling fell out onto the kitchen table.

I was like, 'Well, that looks painful!'

She answered, 'It is. Don't do it!'

But aside from the diary escapade and the boy whom it was written about, I went on to have a very successful ~~sex life~~ relationship with another boy, also a stoner, from when I was about 15 years old until I was around 17. And when I say successful, I mean he only gave me chlamydia once and nearly gave me crabs twice, neither of us died, and my mum always made him stand on the end of every photo so she could cut him out when I dumped him.

She was frothing the day we broke up for the last time. 'The 170th time is a charm' – that's what she said.

By this point in time, we all had mobile phones and not just so our parents could check on us. We'd worked out we, the teen population, could secretly communicate with one another, too. Remember when you used to have to type numbers and letters instead of words so that u cld fit wot u wntd 2 say n 1 txt & not b charged > 10p at a time?

Remember when a ten-pound top-up used to do you a month, and if it didn't, you'd better get the lighter out for smoke signals because there was no way you were getting two top-ups in one month?

Life used to be so simple. LOOK AT US NOW! WHY!

She, the phone rapist, went through my beloved phone when I slept. Rather unfortunately – for me – I slept like I was in a coma, and so she could have drilled through the wall from the outside to get it, and there's a good chance I'd still have slept like a ketamine user. Luckily for her, all she had to do was pull it out gently from under my pillow, like a really creepy bish.

She again found out that I was at risk of making the busy list of pregnant teens in our home city, so she started dropping nuggets of savvy wisdom into our conversations, such as:

- Ejaculation, or jizz as us under-20s called it, was the equivalent calorie intake of four to five doughnuts and was a sure way to get throat-AIDS, as well as fat.

- Ever so gently, on the bus going to my gran's, she informed me that you could get pregnant from giving oral sex – a scrap of disinformation I believed for over a year. It turns out blowjobs are – usually – never life-threatening, fattening, nor able to impregnate.

- Condoms don't offer 100% protection from pregnancy – a grey-area lie, obviously, but she made it seem as if they provided the same level of protection as using a plastic bag held on by an elastic band.

- Anal sex is illegal and will most likely result in AIDS.

All of this came from the woman who'd also told me about 'Smell your mum!' – a defiling strategy that boys used to prove they'd used you like a finger glove.

So, basically, she told me a lot of insanity and I very nearly became a nun. I didn't really have to talk to her about boys, though, because she read all about them on my phone, in my schoolbooks and in my diary.

School

I was capable of so much more than I gave at school. Alright, I was *marginally* more capable of the piss-poor performance I gave at school, and, yes, that is just what adults say when they've left school.

I performed at school like Arnold Schwarzenegger would perform a part in *Sophie's Choice*. Maybe a little worse than that even. You know the old chestnut: 'If I could go back to school, I would in a heartbeat?' That saying makes me want to vomit violently. You would not go back to school! Surely no one would willingly put themselves through the pain and horror of gaggles of hormonal teens again?

School was to me what the iceberg was to the *Titanic*. But ... when I liked a boy, I liked to go.

One boy was put back – not one year, but two – into my year at school. Inevitably, I thought we were in love because he said my name once and was forced to sit beside me in English for a romantic three-week stretch.

I wrote on the inside of my jotter 'MR loves GB 4EVER!!!!!!' and my mum pulled me up about it roughly three love-filled days later. She started out by telling me that I didn't love anyone and that I should 'get a grip' of myself. What she was trying to say was that I wasn't yet at an age where I loved bathing, never mind a 16-year-old boy. I felt she was wrong and my undying love for G. B. would withstand the tests of time.

I was wrong.

Not but a few weeks later, I was 'in love' with another 'bad boy' and so was again frequenting school regularly. I asked my friend – via a note in my own freaking jotter – if she thought I should 'let his D in my V?' to which she replied I definitely should.

She signalled just how great an idea she thought it was by drawing a massive, albeit rudimentary, spurting penis on the opposite page with a love heart around it. It was almost romantic, even with Mrs McDonald's history class as the backdrop.

Thankfully, it wasn't to be. My friend – the drawer of the penis – then went on to sleep with the love of my week, and I was forced to move on. Still, I'm not one to catch on quickly, and so the evidence was left in my jotter. The next time I went to my history class, I found a note from Big Max:

'No, Max. Do not let him enter you. Listen to your mother.
PS. I won't ground you for this. You're welcome.'

Embarrassing? Absolutely. Yep. It was. Overwhelmingly so. I remembering wondering if this was the final straw and she'd no longer love me. Cringe.

Part Three: Things Iraq Torture Techniques Couldn't Get Me to Say to My Mum Ever Again

1. I've lost (insert any item of clothing, including socks, here)

It took roughly 37 hours of mental preparation to get to the point of confession, but if you managed to somehow unannoyingly announce the dreadful loss of something she really, really, really, very passionately cared about, like socks for instance, and delivered the disastrous news at the right tone and pitch, and at an effectual verbal speed, she was less likely to rip you a new one on the spot. It was a learning curve, but reaching enlightenment was a kind of triumph that books should be written about.

I had to do it. There was no escape. The time had come when I had to tell her that I'd lost my school shirt – a terrifying, albeit short, period of my life, which would lead to the need of a bath immediately after and therapy later on.

We were between homes at the time and living either at my gran's or at my aunt's house for the most part, so I was losing my shit faster than 2007 Britney Spears.

I got screamed at so outlandishly violently and whacked on my butt so fiercely that I was forced to try and strangle myself in the comfort of my gran's spare room. I'd thought hard about it and it was in my own emotional best interest to pass away. Financial, too. She'd also just said there'd be no pocket money that week.

Melodramatic? That's a yes from me, but not nearly as dramatic as the point where she walked in and saw me with one hand round my neck and another round my Gameboy (in case you could carry things on with you), and it was apparent I'd wet my chosen deathbed.

The most demeaning part of it all came later that night, when I had to sleep with her on the couch – tops to tails – all because the bed was wet and my ass was sore. But we said no more about it, and that's because when she went into her bag – probably to see if there was something in it to throw at me – she realised she'd already taken my school shirt and I was the victim of misinformation and godawful parenting.

Guiding tip: Sometimes, with parents, you just have to wait them out and hope they make good decisions on their own.

2. I wasn't at school

We'll start with how I managed to skip school so extensively: I wrote a note in my mum's handwriting stating that we'd moved address, and so all the letters that should have made their way to our house on Princes Street ended up in a gyro drop somewhere else in the city (a gyro drop is an empty house that is used by one half of a couple as a place for their mail to be delivered in order to scam extra money from their government, which I endorse, because fuck Parliament).

We'd lived in no fewer than 13 houses by the time we moved into our Princes Street house, so I was no stranger to a gyro drop and their usual locations.

I declared it GYRO DROP CHRISTMAS, which lasted for weeks! It worked a treat. I was enjoying my days like the summer holidays had turned up in February. Then, alas, she got one of her 'feelings'.

I. Really. Hate. Those. Feelings. I want to fight them.

Have you ever heard a parent state that they've just got the 'best feeling' their kid is up to something great? No! Seemingly parents are only tuned in to negativity. It's a terrible affliction that plagues them far too often and should be stamped out, like sadism.

She checked my attendance with the school only to discover it was 100% ... 100% definite that I hadn't attended for three weeks straight. She declared it I'm-gonna-kill-this-little-bastard Christmas, which outshone my own festive period excessively.

We will move on by telling the indisputable truth that I was a little sheltered growing up in many ways, and when I say a little sheltered, I mean it was like living with the Amish. I'm pretty sure she suffered heavily from Overprotective Mother Syndrome. As a result, not only did I believe unicorns were real until I was age 13, and that *The Exorcist* only played if you had a code to say aloud at the beginning of the movie, but I was also unaware that there were free clinics you could go to that helped you should you have had sex and be casually wondering whether or not you had AIDS or any other fruity sounding disease, like lymphogranuloma venereum or syphilis.

Although, thanks to my experience at the doctor's a short time before, I was always feeling apprehensive about any testing. And so started my three-week, and unauthorised, break from school.

My friend, and we remain friends so I won't name her, got a letter from the GUM clinic notifying her that she needed to go in for an appointment because a boy she'd slept with had given her name in what I imagine was a busy list of thrilled females, each with a chance of winning a sexual infection.

But when she told me that the GUM clinic had sent her the letter, I just sat looking at her wondering if I'd caught insta-AIDS, too, because I'd used her toothbrush.

I was like, 'That's rough. Any chance you can ask them to check me out? I heard abscesses are painful as shit.'

She looked back at me as if she was wondering which one of the Teletubbies had been molesting me for the last decade (all bets on Po if we are ever betting on which of them was a paedo).

She didn't seem that excited to explain to me that the GUM clinic was a sexual health clinic and that's where you went when some fool – who did not wrap his tool – had a sexually transmitted disease, and so had added your name to the list of people he'd gotten it from or given it to.

It's actually like the perfect hunting ground for a Bill Cosby type: there's nothing but fragile and vulnerable girls about. He'd have saved a ton of cash on drugs if someone had just told him about Ninewells Hospital in Dundee.

It's a bit like a lottery for the teen clients, too: you might hit the jackpot and end up with AIDS, or you might just end up in the draw that got everyday, common clap.

So, I, at last, understood, and after offering my condolences, I went straight to my mum and stepdad and told them about the conversation. They both laughed at me like I'd told them they were no longer financially responsible for me.

However, my mum did not laugh when she found out I wasn't at school the next week because I'd gone with my anonymous friend to her appointment, and that I hadn't been there the two weeks before that either. She did not laugh at all – there wasn't even a smirk. She looked a lot like Jack Nicholson in *A Few Good Men* actually.

I got the dreaded whisper-shout – the scariest kind – and drop-kicked up the stairs, which is a feat all on its own.

It's the one that fastest brings out the throbbing vein on her head that looks like it gets Down's Syndrome just as it surfaces. My stepdad once said, and I agree, that it is probably the eighth wonder of the world.

3. It's peaceful to drown

My uncle Paul, my mum's brother, was 17 when he drowned in Clatto Park. It's a country park super far north in Dundee. It's also the place a lot of kids used to go to get finger-banged.

I assumed that her brother's death was the reason I wasn't allowed to go there with all the other kids in the summer holidays at nights. Well, that, and she hated me.

My guidance teacher, 'Mrs A' as we affectionately called her (because I can't remember how to spell her name), told us, for a reason that escapes me at present, that it is peaceful to drown – intelligence I passed on to my mum.

She was sat in my aunt Louise's kitchen. There we all were: two equals and me sitting around a wooden picnic bench in her oblong kitchen, talking like two of us were grown-ups and one of us was a Zika baby. And once I – the family imbecile – finished relaying the soothing, consoling information of my uncle's presumably peaceful, albeit watery, death, my mum exploded into a severe, blistering rage that forced my aunt's dog to shit on the linoleum floor and her indoor cat to make a run for it. I just sat looking at her like I'd seen her detachable vagina fall off and concluded that that was how she was able to shout at me like an army major.

When she was finally done telling me how selfish I was, I left.

Okay, that's a lie. Let me rephrase to be more congruent with the actual events: she threw me out, by the shoulder/neck and hair. I might have got a foot to the butthole, too, and then, even after all of that, the death blow came: she told me she'd see me at home.

Nothing more was said on the matter because she'd used her bitch quota for the day. However, at Christmas this year (so, just a short 14 years later), I brought the subject up again just to see how much things have actually changed between us – to find out if she is lying to me about the onset of arthritis and could still take me out like an empty tracksuit.

I broached it lightly like a man trying to hide he was on fire: I told her that it was peaceful to drown, and my stepdad chimed in backing me up, and she took it rather well.

She was all, 'Aw, well, that's actually nice to hear …'

You know what's not peaceful? Getting thrown out your aunt's house and having to walk the eight miles home as it rains with one sore cheek and bruised dignity, and then having to hide in your room for learning at school.

She did say to me that Christmas I was never to watch someone drown. We are all still trying to work out what she meant. I was like, 'Well, yeah, it wasn't really my dream to …'

Dogs have never had a war, so who are the real animals?

#peopleresh*t

4. I didn't take the dog to the pound

To be honest, all I wanted was a dog I could ride around the house like a dinosaur, but she was petrified of all animals, and dogs in particular. What a pansy. God, Reynolds, you can wrestle men in and out of nightclubs, but you're scared of Yorkies. You've got to wonder.

She used to make me cross the road with her if one was on the same side of the street as us, even if it had a muzzle, two back wheels and no teeth and had recently undergone a taxidermy session. So when we finally got Scruffy, my incontinent yet awesome dog, I was elated. He was great except for the fact she went and picked him up from the pound herself. She picked the most fudged-up dog she could find and declared that she would take care of him until he irritated her so much by doing the things that the pound had already told her he was going to do that she no longer harboured the will to care about him at all. For the love of all things peed-on, though, I loved that dog.

He urinated at the exact moment you brought him back in from a walk and ball-barfed at some very inconvenient times. He also barked when you left him alone in the house, like a drug dog sniffing El Chapo, but he was also a legend of mass proportions. I mean, the dog liked porn! Any time you switched to Channel 5 after 9 p.m., there was nothing but savage hand-pumping showing.

Scruffy would immediately look at the TV and show us all his little lipstick D. It was kind of hilarious and proved to be a popular party trick.

Hopefully, his owners before us knew that dogs were meant for life and not for fucking, because I hate to think that Scruffy was an abuse victim. I hope he was either really weird or a cute old man trapped inside a dog's body.

One day, Big Max was in a particularly bad mood that I'm confident Freud couldn't explain, and she decided that was the day Scruffy was going. She'd threatened it long enough, and his mounting sins were just too high and precariously balanced.

He'd apparently tried to spy on her as she got out of the bath (a point for the old-man theory); he'd pissed on the bathroom floor so that when she got out, she slipped, fell backwards and slammed her head against the tiles; and he'd pissed on her rug, too – and all in one week. So, it wouldn't have looked good for Scruffy even if he'd been able to shit out gold bricks. There was really no saving him.

She cast me and the poor, half-blind, half-bladdered dog out onto the streets and told me in no uncertain terms he was to go back to the dog pound and I was to come back and not moan, cry or look sad about it. So, naturally, I went to my gran's house. A safe haven. A place where a really old, wise woman agreed with all the things I said.

Alas, Stella told me she wasn't allowed to have pets in her building, so I was shit out of luck with that plan.

I waited a few hours before I took myself and the dog back home. On the long walk there, I told Scruffy he could attack her if he wanted, but I think he was going deaf too, because he just lay down when we returned to the dreaded Theatre of Horrors, as I'd nicknamed our 14th house. She let it slide, and Scruffy lived to see another day wherein he was shouted at for pissing on the hall carpet again.

5. You didn't take the dog to an adoption farm

But then this happened: I went to my auntie's for the day, and now that I think about it, she was probably in on the whole disgusting, painful, appalling, harrowing, tragic affair.

Upon returning home that night, my mum told me that she'd taken Scruffy to an adoption farm.

She painted a beautiful scene for me: she told me that he was running wild and free with the horses and pissing on the grass like he owned it.

She went on to tell me of butterflies and meadows and how she was sure he'd regained partial sight after the unbridled joy he'd experienced just in sniffing his new surroundings.

She even told me about how his tail had wagged at her, as if to say, 'Goodbye and thank you' in some sort of dog Morse code.

Now, I've believed a lot of dumb and insane things in my life, but if you think I'd believe something like this, you'd be absolutely right.

The only thing I couldn't believe was that she'd done something like that for me. It really took me a long time to accept she'd gone out of her way to do something so monumentally beautiful for both Scruffy and me.

Bittersweet, but great and beautiful. It soothed me to think of him happy and free, without limits, roaming like the beast his gentle soul had always wanted to be.

Hook. Line. Sinker.

The next week, I returned to school after the summer holidays had ended and told all of my friends that my mum had taken my dog to a fancy adoption farm and that I was recovering well from the trauma. None of them listened, but it was cathartic nonetheless. I finished my first day back at school, walked outside the main gates, and who did I see? Scruffy!

I was thinking, *Oh my god! They even have a chauffeur service and field trips!*

He was standing with his tail wagging like someone was waving sausages in his face and the delightful aroma was sending him into a frenzy.

The traumas:

1. He was gleefully awaiting George, a boy from my class, and was watching him approach. Turns out the dry-haired little mongrel could see over medium to long distances after all.

2. George's mum, the lady holding Scruffy back from attacking George with meaty-flavoured kisses, informed me, while snot and tears filled my face in equal measure, that Scruffy was in the dog pound and she'd retrieved him hoping to give him a good home because he looked so miserable in there – a lot like he'd been abandoned. I hope to whatever gods may exist that she didn't pick George's dad the way she picked dogs.

3. I got grounded and verbally abused when I went home and called my mum a monster for tricking me with Scruffy.

I was locked out and so waiting at the top of the steps for her, which gave me ample time to think of all the things I was going to yell at her so that she'd fall to the ground and beg for forgiveness.

After a couple of false alarms and a few weirded-out neighbours, she arrived, and I wailed that she was a liar and a barbarian and that I hated her. It worked … in the exact opposite way I'd planned. She threw her bag to the floor and then took two stairs at a time towards me. She told me that was no way to talk to her and that if I 'weren't such a sensitive little bastard', she would have told me the truth in the first place. She then sent me to my room and told me to think about what I'd said and done, while jabbing me in the back and kicking me in the calves – both preferable to the emotional trauma I was undergoing at the time.

Guiding tip: Guilt can make grown-ups act in the strangest ways. It's best to bide your time. If they fudge you off, wait five to ten years to bring it up. They are usually sorrier by then.

6. Can I stay out later? … The bus was late

This was a dark, dark, horrendous period in our mother–daughter relationship. She refused to believe just about anything I said, including, but not limited to, that I was hungry, tired, thirsty, alive, sad, happy, at school; that she was a shit mum; that I wasn't taking drugs; that I didn't know the dealer who'd just been arrested in Fife; that I wasn't stealing from her, or from shops; that my friends weren't gang leaders; that my friends weren't on heroin; that I wasn't on heroin; that I didn't spend my bus money on drugs; etc., etc., etc.

She was becoming a real drag.

I believe I did know better than to ask to stay out later than permitted. Somewhere deep down in me, I think that knowledge did exist, but I just never used it. In fact, one time I asked to stay out later and she told me to come home earlier.

I made my way home on the bus – the earlier bus – but it was attacked by the Hilltown 'gang', known locally as the Young Hilltown Huns. They smashed the windows with stones and bricks and threw some other particularly unpleasant items in its direction. Needless to say, I arrived home later than I was supposed to on account of waiting for the police to show up and 20 passengers and me being decanted to another bus.

I got home and was immediately summoned to the living room. She was sat in her usual seat and in her usual 'I'm about to fuck you up' pose.

I tried to explain what had happened, and she said something about my imagination and how much time I was going to have with it when I was grounded for the next month. For love nor money, that woman wouldn't just accept that something could have happened that had slowed my speedy return from happiness to home.

It wasn't until I took my coat off and glass fell out that she really took notice.

She took the evidence and came to the only rational conclusion possible: at 14, I was moonlighting as a robber. I'd obviously been breaking into shops or homes, and this was the evidence, which she would be taking to the police. She then annoyingly punctuated her fury-filled rant with: 'Make no mistake about it. I'll be going to the station tomorrow!'

Even when she heard the next day via Tay FM, the city's local radio station, that an event identical to the one I'd told her about had happened at roughly the exact time I said – even upon considering all the facts – she still concluded I was definitely lying and a mastermind of petty crime.

7. Can you stop smoking so I can have dinner money?

I wouldn't say this to Big Max again if it was set to cure AIDS.

My sweet little grandma was always on my side, no matter what! Come rain or shine, Big Max in a good mood or Big Max in a bad mood, Stella was always on my team. She was one of those grans who thought that if I got in trouble, it was my friend's fault; even if I was alone and caught on

CCTV and admitted it, she'd *still* find a way to exonerate me. God bless grannies.

However, it seemed like the devil may have been on the prowl. As we know, all good things must come to an end. And as we also know, smokers are selfish bastards. It seemed she wanted her daughter to have cancer, because she didn't want her to quit smoking. When I told my little old Stella that she should tell Big Max to quit for the good of our economy and my love of lunchtime chip-shop buys, she nearly had an old-person stroke. It was our first and last disagreement, and it hurt.

Walloping regret clung to me for days as I grappled with the fear my gran would now take my mum's side more than mine.

My mum told me in no uncertain terms to 'FUCK OFF', too, because I was the beneficiary of free school dinners. But the problem was that cool people didn't eat there. They left the school, went to the shops and got a fritter roll.

She said that if I really didn't want to go to the school's dinner hall and eat with all the rest of the poor people, I had two options:

1. Sell the dinner ticket. (Was she high as well as at risk of cancer? Who would be stupid enough to buy their way from coolness to cafeteria by buying dinner tickets and eating the cook's dick hairs?)

2. Starve.

Guiding tip: Uncover stealth-mode options whenever possible ...

3. **The secret bonus option:** spend a lot of time persuading her to take a bath, and then, with the precision of a jewel thief robbing the Met, 'borrow' 50p at a time. The obstacles I used to have to hurdle just to get a fried tatty and a 10p roll!

8. You're embarrassing me!

The most embarrassing times were generally those when she hit me in front of people. Any people: family, strangers, her friends, my friends, shopkeepers. I was also not a fan of being shouted at in front of people. But one time, she made me cry so much that my skin had salt stains for a week after.

My friends and I were in my aunt's back garden re-enacting scenes from the PlayStation game 'Alien' with the aid of dog fences, sheds, stones, poles and egg cartons. It was going great right up until Big Max showed up and stole the show.

She probably heard me have fun all the way from our house, just a short three miles up the road, and immediately made her way to me to kill it dead.

Without any provocation, she took an opportunity to be an insufferable show-off and went for an easy target: my ability to pull off the quality look of a London teenage boy.

As the nuggets of abuse came hurling in thicker and faster, I made the mistake of showing her my pain. Like blood in the water for a shark, it made her all the hungrier for my 12-year-old soul's happiness.

I shouted, 'Stop it! You're embarrassing me!'

Her reaction to this comment included howling with laughter, turning around, bending over and giving me the finger via her arsehole.

I threw myself to the ground so as not to make any more eye contact with her vicious anal cavity, covered thinly by her abhorrent pink skirt, and she laughed herself all the way into the house while my friends laughed furiously at me.

And so the tip is: Never let your abuser know that they're a c*nt until you can outwit them.

9. Your butt jiggles like jelly

It was like watching a kitten die. All I said through a giggle was that her butt jiggled like 'Gran's Christmas jelly', and as she turned her head over her shoulder to look down at me walking behind her on the stairs, I witnessed a small piece of her inner confidence crumble into ash.

Her butt did jiggle, though, mainly because she walks like she's got a club foot when she's forced into any sort of exercise, including climbing stairs. She walked up stairs like a slinky was going to chase her up them.

The stairs where this canny observation took place were the narrow, steep stairs from my aunt's dining room to her daughter's attic rooms.

She says it could have made a lesser woman anorexic, something I bet she wished she was in her 40s when her metabolism slowed to a snail's pace.

I also told all of my friends she sounded like a machine gun when she walked up the stairs farting, too. As it stands, she still vehemently denies the allegation, but I had to get her back somehow for giving me the one-up through her legs and via her arsehole.

Classic mother–daughter duo.

10. You don't suit that fringe!

There she was in her bedroom, standing by the mirror with a pair of scissors in her hand. I happened to walk by and casually observe her awkward stance. I looked at her face, searching it, hoping that there was no indication on it that the scissors were about to be used on something I loved. But the fear soon took a deep dive back down to its usual resting place at the bottom of my tummy as utter joy replaced it in my heart: her face looked like a football.

She'd cut herself the most heinous of thick fringes. It looked like she'd gotten a half bowl cut.

I was forced to unceremoniously spit out my cheddar quiche, which, looking back, might have had bits of 'vegetarian' bacon in it.

I cried out aghast, 'Ewww! You do not suit that!', pointing to her now curtained forehead.

Some mothers would've asked for a second opinion, while others might've told their *expressive* and *honest* child to go away.

Mine, however, opted for a more hostile comeback: she summoned the Hitler arm, pointed to my own pimple-prone forehead and growled, 'Yeah, well, you should have one with a forehead that size!' She then proceeded to use both of her hands to mark a space in the air that she felt was representative of my forehead's volume. But she sized it as if I was wearing the fridge as a hat.

Fourteen-year-old me was forced to ask my stepdad if it did indeed look like I had Down's syndrome, to which he calmly replied, 'Not to me.' But I swear his eyes stopped about a foot higher than where I thought my head ended.

She then slammed her bedroom door shut and shouted through it that I could 'fuck off'.

The following night when I saw her, she had a side shade and a lot − *a lot* − of contouring.

11. I know who my dad is ...

... And I thought he was Jesus.

We were making our way to my auntie Jenny's house so we could be free of one another when we got to Sandy's paper shop. There's a good chance the fat bastard in me had sprung to life and I'd started begging for chocolate, but my appetite soon left as out walked a man wearing flip-flops, which served to prompt my memory.

Pulling excitedly on my mum's hand, I tilted my head up and enthusiastically told her the one thing in life that could've given her an under-30s stroke: 'Mum, I know who my dad is! I've been seeing him!'

She stopped dead. She actually looked like a cardboard cut-out of herself singing an Adele song. I was like, 'Mum ... Mummy?', and tugged on her sleeve a few more times.

Like most other kids, I'd been drilled on what to do if you went to your mum's bedroom in the morning and she wouldn't wake up (Sundays didn't count); I was a wee bit lost when it came to freezing mid-stride in the street, so I turned to go into Sandy's and ask for a Twix while I waited it out.

Finally, she looked down at five-year-old me and said, 'Okay, what does this man look like, and where have you been seeing him?'

I'm not the sharpest tool in the box at the best of times – I always pull the doors labelled push, and drawing stick men with heinously disproportioned body parts was my crowning moment in school – but this, this I clicked onto pretty fast.

I answered her truthfully, but like a short, evil genius: 'I see him every day at school.'

'Okay,' she said, trying to brush the irritation and fear from her voice, 'what does this man look like, and what does he say?'

The jig was up, the charade was over. I wasn't going to be able to make Jesus fit into Gary's mould. I hadn't developed that talent yet.

I moved forward, sadly, with the truth: 'He's got long brown hair, he wears sandals, and he has a blue cape and blue eyes. Everyone says he's a fishmonger.'

'Jesus?'

'Yeah, but I'm sure you told me his name is Gary!'

Children are great, aren't they? No one knows why they push you towards adopting them out, but they do and they are good at it.

Oh, how we laughed about this. Ten years later ... when her heartbeat had returned to normal and we were both stout atheists.

12. I've been swapping the painkillers out with your medicine

Alas, she didn't get a good mental illness like Hank in *Me, Myself and Irene*. She got bipolar, and it sucked harder than a Thai mail-order bride going for a pair of Louboutins.

She was supposed to take her medicine every day, but somehow she'd come to the conclusion that the tablets, and not the extra food she was eating, would make her fat, and so she chose not to take them.

And we all lived happily and fat-free after ... apart from me and her.

In another genius move, I made the unprecedented decision to swap the paracetamol we had under the cutlery drawer out with her bipolar meds that were stacking up in her room.

Relax. You can't drug someone already taking drugs. You can only surprise them.

Surprise, Ma! You're fixed, but you'll keep the headache!

What could possibly go wrong?

In a massive plot twist, she found out, and when she did, she looked like Pablo Escobar finding out his stash was really sherbet.

13. I don't know how all my presents got tears in the paper!

It was a dark, dark time.

No, literally – it was a dark few moments that saw me round the armchair and squeeze behind the cupboard door in the living room to feast my eyes on the wonders Big Max had hidden there.

Big Max had uttered six Christmas-ruining words: 'Don't go looking around the house.'

BINGO. There was a secret to be found. 'Get me the binoculars and the lube, high places and small spaces are about to be searched!'

Mums, dads, all people reading: don't do it. Swallow the urge. They will search and they will find. There've been less thorough police searches for missing people.

Big Max let it out. She failed us both when she inadvertently set me off on a quest to ruin 25 December 1997 – forever (she still brings it up).

And on this glorious day, when I rounded the chair with my grandad's Poundstretcher torch strapped to my head and prised open the door, I winced as its reflection off of the iridescent wrapping paper nearly blinded me, and then I welled up.

She'd done it: she'd bought me a Furby. I was emotionally overcome. She'd bought me something I wanted and not just something she wanted me to have.

The other thing was, I didn't actually know the Furby was in there.

I had a feeling.

I had to do my preteen self a solid and confirm. Obvz.

With that oath in mind, I began tearing small to medium-sized holes in each of the presents, not really bothering to discriminate based on size and the logic that a four-foot box probably wasn't a Furby.

Alas, a time comes in every girl's life when she has to 'fess up and own her actions and their consequences, and this was definitely, absolutely not that time. But it happened anyway.

All I had to do was ***look*** at the cupboard the following day. It afforded her the opportunity to notice the white leather armchair had moved two inches – so, like a mile to an OCD person – and she shot up, grabbed the leather chair and tossed it aside like dolly furniture.

I winced, wondering if she was definitely going to work out it was me.

She flung open the cupboard door. At the same moment in time, I shot across the room like I was about to shit myself, which I was.

The next thing I remember was looking at my pinky finger, the first part of my body to reach the door and its handle, thinking, *Are you joking? I never ask you to do anything!* It hadn't been strong enough to catch the handle properly. It had doomed us.

Just then, Big Max swooped in on me from above like a bird of prey and hung me upside down from the ankle. My ass was beaten like a second-hand drum, which served as a great drum roll for the announcement that Christmas was cancelled. Gone. Just like that.

Afterwards, I was to treat that cupboard like we treated Gary and Jesus: like it didn't exist.

It was touch and go for a while, but we went ahead with Christmas when it dawned on her she couldn't return all of the gifts I'd already opened and poked holes in.

Guiding statement: Name a greater law than that of returns ... There isn't one.

Imagine someone told child-you that one day your punishments would be your adult interests,
like going to bed early, not leaving your house on the weekends and getting socks as gifts ...

14. It's ridiculous. Just get a black carpet!

~~I'll start by saying I am still completely unable to comprehend the flawed logic this woman operated through.~~ I'll start by saying Big Max was partially retarded in some ways.

After a period of being homeless for a few months, we got what was to be a long-term home. It was the house where the hallway and bathroom were bigger than my room – I don't mean you had to combine them for that calculation to add up; I mean that, even in isolation, some moron had made it so that the bathroom was bigger than my bedroom, as was my mum's bedroom cupboard and every other room in the whole disproportionate, largely screwed-up house.

Big Max is a dab hand at the ole decor game. But she's not to be trusted unless you can float. What she lacks is the mundane principle known to most people over the age of seven as logic. We got a white carpet in our new house. We got a white carpet in an OCD, bipolar person's house. We got a white carpet in the first part of the house you entered. The only part of the house you couldn't avoid. She got one in a house in which you weren't permitted to sit on any part of the sofa on which a cushion or pillow was resting, lest it be creased or unfluffed (that is a word, don't lie). The same house where the tins of food all faced due south and a cardinal offence was stepping on the rug, which lay *conveniently* in the centre of the living room. You were to walk around that rug to seat yourself on the sofa (the sofa that you were not permitted to use for back support), which was adjacent to the curtains that weren't to be closed because they weren't curtains as much as they were hanging material meant to be swooned at.

So, again, she got us a white carpet in the hallway that Martha Stewart couldn't have kept clean. It was an unprecedented level of fuckery, even for Big Max. Nonetheless, no one wants to fight with a lunatic, so we all tried. That meant you were to open the door to our house and levitate across the hallway into the living room. Surely, if any of us that lived at 197 Princes Street, apartment F, were able to suspend ourselves in mid-air or fly even short distances, we'd use that power to glide up the stupendous amount of stairs we had to climb first or, and more likely, out the living-room window when we sensed an adult tantrum coming on.

We didn't start out trying to solve the problem of the now ombré carpet by getting a doormat and wiping our feet on the way in ... No, no, no! Doormats were dirty and not worth the money, according to one of us residing at the house at the time. Take a magical, wild guess as to which one of us ...

We started out trying to solve this unique issue by taking our shoes off at the door, but Scotland is deathly cold in winter, so that was eventually vetoed when my stepdad nearly lost a foot to frostbite. Then she bought a transparent cover for about one square foot of the carpet. Why not enough to cover it all, you might wonder? We wonder that too.

When it all became too much for me, and thinking about my footprint on the carpet leading to a handprint on my frost-bitten face was taking up too much of my time, I finally worked up the courage to confront her.

I said, 'Just get a f*cking black carpet, Goddammit, Max!' (The 'f*cking' was in my head, obviously.)

The response was unimaginable. That wheezing bag of misery sentenced me to an indefinite living-room ban. I was to cross the hallway's expanse in **one** lunge and go straight to my room from now on. It was blissful. Blissful's twin sister – Merriment – was right there in my six-by-six-foot room, too.

Guiding tip: Approach parents cautiously. Don't be afraid of punishments, as sometimes they are secretly the opposite.

Part Four: My Mum on the Importance of ...

Tea/dinnertime

Mum: 'You'll come home for your dinner.'
    Me: 'I can eat later or when I'm out!'
    The above, loosely coined 'conversation' took place on more occasions than I've had hot dinners in my adult lifetime.

When the importance vanished

We are lovers of clothes. Material possessions make us feel happier than holidays. We like to have something to stay thin for and sometimes get thin for. We like thinking about what we might wear when we get thin, and we accept gift cards to clothing retailers readily. We also enjoy the feeling of thinking someone we dislike will see us in an outlandishly perfect outfit, and it will ruin their day. Potentially two days if the right outfit is perfectly embracing us.

    When I was about fourteen years old, I was complaining about not having enough clothes to hang off of my man-like frame. My mum said, 'We can have good clothes, or we can have good food.'

We were at a point in time where we were pouring the unused milk from our cereal bowls back into the milk jug after agreeing not to drink the excess anymore. We were getting thin and saving money. Teamwork makes the dream work!

Having cool threads AND still having Weetabix for two out of three meals sounded right up our street.

With a look and a nod, we both agreed on the good clothes. Bravo on the 14 years of painful pretending, though, Big Max!

Once my friend Raquel asked me if my mum was a prostitute because I 'always had smart clothes on', and I semi-let her believe it because I refused to admit that we shopped at TK Maxx. Now I'd organise a human rights march if they shut it down.

Being in a routine

Mum: 'It's good to be in a routine! It stops you from acting like a little bastard! You're going to have to start staying less at Gran's and Auntie Jenny's house, too!'

Me: 'What! Why? No way! Why do you hate meeeeee?'

When the importance vanished

When we became homeless.

   Mum: 'You're going to have to stay with Gran and Auntie J. more often until we get a house!'

Not smoking

Mum: 'If I have the slightest inkling you're smoking, young lady, all your money stops and I'll make you smoke 20 in a row.'

   Me: 'Never gonna happen, smoking is for losers!'

When the importance vanished

When I called smokers losers and she realised she could easily smoke 40 a day.

Exercise

Mum: 'Exercise is one of the most important things you can do for yourself. It's like medicine.'

   Me: 'I know! I'm going to take PE as one of my fifth-year subjects.'

When the importance vanished

When she refused to let me take it as a subject at school in fifth year.

Surgery

Mum (looking at the TV in disbelief): 'Max, promise me you will never get surgery!'

    Me (looking at the TV in disbelief): 'Mum, I don't think I ever, ever, ever will.'

When the importance vanished

When she thought I had my dad's huge nose and fivehead. She asked my auntie Jenny the following (in front of me): 'Jenny, if she doesn't grow into her head and nose by the time she's 18, can we borrow the money for surgery? She can't go around like that!'

    Take a second to process that. I had teeth like pretzels and one squint eye, I was born with meningitis, and I have a heart murmur, but she was worried about my fivehead and nose and people knowing I was hers.

    It's why I love her. She gets me. Fight us, we're vain.

Not dressing like a lesbian

Me: 'I love my tracksuit bottoms. I think I want a pair for every day when I grow up, and you know how you told me that if you die, you want to be buried in your catsuit? Well, if I die, I want to be buried in my trackies!'

Mum: 'You'll grow out of them, or you'll be ripped out of them! And you can bet your tracksuits will be buried before you!'

When the importance vanished

Never. I once got a shell tracksuit from my gran: it was a matching jacket and bottoms in a glorious night-sky navy, which had three white-hot stripes on each side. As far as I know, tracksuits are worn by athletes, lawbreakers, juvenile delinquents and Eminem: I looked like an athlete. A fashionable Olympian, some would say. The paragon of sporty elegance might be another term coined and thrown at me if you were to have observed me that beautiful June night in 2002. A modern-day muse and Adidas-adorned superstar in what seemed that day like a town full of drably dressed Dundonians.

You know those days when whatever introspective life you're living is reflected back at you in the eyes of everyone whom you catch looking at you? The days you feel good, or bad, or perhaps feel fat, ugly, or maybe hot, and so you become sure everyone you walk by is looking at you as if they are thinking the exact same things about you – those days? Well, boarding the No. 29 bus from Charleston to take a whirlwind tour of the lower half of the city, and upon eventually reaching our house just outside the city centre, I was more positive than a proton that everyone was looking at me because I looked like a Milan tracksuit model.

Usually, I would sit at the very back of the bus, but that day I chose to sit at the very front, in the spaces that had adjacent signs urging people sitting there to give the seat to OAPs or parents with buggies if need be. Usually, I was a vehement opponent of such a prejudiced system. It preyed on the seated rather than those with walking aids on which to lean. This day, though, I willed it to happen.

I pictured myself leaping up from the seat and short-lunging to the centre of the bus's aisle where all of my travelling companions would be able to bask in the glory of my new navy threads.

The way the shiny shell coat in all of its splendour hung off of my breastless, man-like frame must have been an artist's dream, and the matching bottoms gathered in at the ankles were giving my silhouette the illusion of a shape (the shape of an exclamation mark). I'm honestly shocked no one fainted at the sight of my sumptuousness.

I got off the bus, gave the keen onlookers a little wave and a nod of my tall forehead, festooned with pimples brought to life by the contrast between their reddish hue and the crisp navy of my most prized possession. And those people on the bus, they didn't wave back, and that was probably because they were still in awe.

Imagine I'd swindled my gran out of the cash for new trainers and a cap. There'd have been a riot! That tracksuit was a fireball all of its own though. I just gave it somewhere to hang.

I proceeded to my house, satisfied in the knowledge that I had shown a decent amount of appreciation for their infatuated looks with that one small wave as I stepped off the bus, the sweeping swagger now carrying me effortlessly homeward.

I swankily entered our warm, safe, mock-free house. My mother erupted into a colourful fit of laughter, ranging from small self-choking giggles to howling and grunting. I believe there were tears of joy as she noted the white socks that poked out from under my suit's ankle grips. She tried to say something about me and a Michael Jackson, but she couldn't catch her breath in time to get it all out. Unfortunately, we will never know what compliment she wished to pay me because the moment has gone ... and will stay in the past.

She then proceeded to call my aunt and boast of the tracksuit's talking points. They moved on to something else quickly, because they just laughed for the next 20 to 30 minutes of the call.

My love for tracksuit bottoms will never fade or die, nor will my No. 29-bus Style Icon status.

Guiding tip: Tracksuits aren't just for exercising and can be used in polite society. See Kim Kardashian's style circa 2018 for proof!

Parents are for feeding you and paying for your clothing. They are not known for their fashion sense; therefore, they, and their Hawaiian-looking shirts, are to be ignored on all things fashion.

Part Five: What My Mum Did When I ...

Asked her if she was sure someone would want to marry me when I was older

I was probably around five foot when I asked her if she was sure someone would want to marry me when I was 'older and pretty', just like she'd promised me I would be. I was already feeling quite dejected, because I'd *kind of* asked a boy out from school, and he'd definitely said no.

Okay, what actually happened was that I sat next to a boy in English class for a week to see if he was all, 'Max, that's a great sharpener you have there, any chance I can stick my pencil in it?' Or maybe – I mused – he would start with, 'What a glorious-looking, unmarked white rubber you have there. Any chance you want to rub it on my shaft drawings in Techy class?' I'd have also settled for 'Hello', but he just moved seats to sit by a far less stationery-centric student. In other words, he was a c*nt.

We were standing in the kitchen while my mum cooked some truly heinous concoction that let her serve me soup one night and the little bits of beef in it as stew the next. And when I'd said the words, 'Are you sure someone will want to marry me when I'm older, Mum?' in a tone that conveyed my terror at being alone or, worse, trapped with her until I was 50 years old, she pivoted as if she'd been lying the whole time about the onset of arthritis in her hips.

Holding the spoon in her man-arm as though it was a spear she was readying to plunge into my chest, she snapped, 'What would you want to be married for? Stick in at school and get a good job, you'll never need a man! God, they are useless anyway, Max!'

She continued, 'And no one is going to marry a girl that bathes but just once a week! Jesus Christ! Listen to more Destiny's Child and less Celine Dion,' she let out, finally at ease with how exasperated I'd just made her feel.

Obviously, I did go on to get married that one time, and he'd probably welcome your commiseration letters. It turns out I'm not *always* as easy a wife as teen-me thought I'd be.

In my defence, one time he said he liked Trump, and if we were going to the airport, he made me get there four hours early – that sort of stuff is really weighing on a relationship.

Oh yeah, and currently he's trying to divorce me, but I don't want to just now, so we are having a marital stand-off. I'll let you know if I've had to kill him because he cheated me of my prime years and is pushing me back out onto the dating scene with a Tinder profile that reads 'Enthusiastic (= *annoying*), like eating out (= *can't cook*). I look like J-Law (= *if she survived a shark attack*).'

Captain's log: Hindsight – 23 February 2019

Weddings and grooms seem to be a sore point in our family. Big Max herself nearly fell out with my gran because she'd refused to buy her a wedding dress and 'Rent-a-Groom' plus a photographer for her 30th birthday.

She'd said she had no interest in *actually* being married, not to mention her and my stepdad were on another small holiday from their relationship again, meaning she was shit out of luck on cutting costs via the groom, but she wanted the photos ... I, honest-to-any-god, wondered whether or not I really was in *The Truman Show* many, *many* times.

However, by some miraculous miracle, Adam and Big Max eventually got married – a short 21 years after starting up. Sure, they had a few hiatuses ranging from short to moderately long in time, one of them had a baby in one little break, the other had kittens when she found out about the other's baby, but, eventually, they committed.

After they'd been wed, we went to New Orleans on their honeymoon (it's not creepy, it's cute), where my now 'official' stepdad got mugged as I slept soundly. The buffoon tried to buy weed on a street corner that El Chapo wouldn't have trodden; my mum – already 467/10 drunk – had to be held back from wreaking utter devastation on anyone in NOLA who so much as looked like a pot dealer. So literally no one in NOLA was safe. She said something about slaughtering 'the bastard' who outsmarted her husband.

The next day, we all missed our early morning flight because Kate and Gerry McCann couldn't quite make it out of bed.

As they lay there, newly married, telling me about their first *adventure* as a married couple, I thought to myself, *Wow, they really are a team now. My hope in life, love and marriage has been reignited.*

Then, as previously mentioned, my own husband tried to divorce me. So, again, **sucker-punched.** And there's a good chance I'll be with a lot of cats by the time I'm 50. Can't wait.

Guiding tip: Like my grandma, Stella, always said: 'Men are like the bus: you miss one, another one is right around the corner. Unless you're a tart, then you'll end up walking.'

– Stella Reynolds, spitting bare truths until 2018.

Forgot my key

I tried everything to keep a key: I hid it at the front door every morning, just down where the skirting didn't meet flush with the wall, which went swimmingly until she found out and said that it was possibly the worst idea anyone had ever had since her own to go through with her pregnancy. Hi, that's me.

I wore it on one of the large hoop earrings I sported for a while in a bid to get people at school to believe I was as cool as Alicia Keys. Didn't work.

Afterwards, I resolved to give it to the receptionist at school every morning so I couldn't lose it, and then generally forgot to pick it up again each night, which meant I would be stood at my front door waiting for my stepdad to get home, as usual.

This is probably the opportune moment to point out that it was a rarity Big Max wasn't actually in the house after I finished school. However, she refused to answer the buzzer, and even when I climbed over the back fence to find that the back door to the building was open, she still wouldn't open the front door to our flat because she was 'teaching me a lesson'. No one knows the lesson intended. It's not important. What's important is that we recognise it seemed a lot like she marginally hated me.

One day, I climbed over the back fence and my new jacket caught on a massively inconvenient splinter. I heard a rip and wondered if that was going to be the same sound my arsehole made when she volleyed her foot up it.

When I finally gained entry to the house that was supposedly 'just as much mine as it was hers', I gave the game up in about 0.489 seconds flat. I immediately shed the puffy garment and hung it up in the hallway cupboard.

The feeling strikes back

I strode into the living room exuding faux calm. Just as I entered, I heard the words, 'Take off your shoes and ...'

'Yeah, that's right, couch bully! You yellow-bellied thunder c*nt, this teen bitch is one step ahead of you, so simmer.' (Obviously, a thought and not an actual sentence uttered aloud – I didn't have an *actual* death wish.)

Faux calm as impetus, I sat directly in the middle of the sofa so as not to ruffle any feathers (in the cushions or otherwise), and then I looked at the TV and avoided eye contact with her at all costs.

'I've got a feeling you're up to something!'

With both eyebrows climbing up my forehead and my shoulders closing in on my chin, I cannily retorted, 'Well, I'm not, so ...'

I know, the Comeback Queen strikes again.

She pounced up from the sofa and rounded on me. She looked me square in the one eye that wasn't squinting from holding in the lie that was liable to get me murder-punched.

'You *never* take off your coat and shoes first thing ...' And with that, she took off through the door and headed for the hall cupboard.

I heard a shoe – presumably mine – clatter off of the opposite cupboard's front and so knew she'd eliminated them from the investigation. But then I heard her knee crack, as they often do when people over 30 stand up, and I knew she was onto the coat. It would only be a matter of time before I had to plead guilty and accept my sentence.

I thought about caterwauling from the window to catch the attention of any police or even criminals in the area, but she was back in before I'd had a chance to properly formulate it.

'What the fuck is this? I just bought you this coat!' she said, holding it up at head height with one hand and pointing to and fro between me and it with the other. 'What happened?'

'It caught on the back.' *No! Wait, I should DEFINITELY NOT connect this with the missing key ...*

Too late.

'I've told you time and time again about that key! That's it! I'm locking the back door every day now, so you're going to have to sit outside on the street until you either remember your keys or someone else lets you in!'

'So I can't play out on the street in case there's a paedophile nearby, but I can sit on it because you won't answer the buzzer?'

'Yes!' she spat violently. I think a bit of her spittle might have landed on my face, as did the sleeve of the coat when she swung it at me repeatedly moments after.

To an onlooker, we would have looked like we were playing competitive hopscotch as I jounced and jerked from foot to foot, bobbing and weaving my way across the living room and away from the now violent garment's reach. The zip caught me on the side of the eye, and so I threw myself to the floor like I was having a seizure and started screaming that I hoped she was ready for a pet, because I was definitely going to be getting a guide dog now. Unfortunately, the zip didn't get me in the cornea, just the lash line as my eye snapped shut.

REFLEXES, NO! BAD!

The next day, she made me buy her a puncture repair kit out of my pocket money, and she patched the coat over its near-fatal gash. *She so good to me.*

Other times, when I knew she was in and I really needed to pee or it was deliriously cold, I would call through the letterbox in a whisper, hopeful that my low, soothing voice would be carried on the wind and the message that I was home and outside would be delivered to her ears like a gentle fairy tale.

Then, of course, she'd throw open the door and I would pretend to frantically search my bag and throw out phrases like: 'So much homework in here! So many praising reports! Can't find that damn key!'

Sometimes it worked, and I was permitted access easily, and other times she was like Gandalf, all, 'You shall not pass!', but with a much better moustache and cleaner whites.

We used to argue about the problem of a lost key a lot, too. She thought we'd be robbed and the insurance wouldn't cover it because we wouldn't be able to prove that we'd been broken into (given the perpetrator would have a key), which was bullshit, because (a) we didn't have any insurance, and (b) there was absolutely no way to identify the key as ours. Duh!

Case closed.

Until we got robbed.

I came home one day, and the door was open, and Big Max was standing in the now very bare hallway. They'd even taken the carpet. She was stood tapping her foot, hands on hips, and with a pained expression etched onto her face that showed no signs of retreating.

'We've been robbed, and, guess what, they had a key!'

Silence.

In my mind, I had a small funeral for my dignity and freedom and bid them farewell. But I replied with, 'Are you sure it was my key?'

She started to laugh uncontrollably. Finally, she snorted out, 'Just kidding, we're getting a new carpet. Makes you think, though, eh!'

Whatabish – that's Latin, for 'what a bitch'.

Guiding tip: When you see their house key unattended, ~~steal~~ relocate it from their key ring to any place else. Watch them flail.

Said flies might be sending me messages

We were lying in her bed, and she was going through a phase of buying old light fixtures made from materials like cast iron and other alternative shite.

We were pretty used to her weekend-millionaire schemes, like when she was planning to iron the whole of Dundee's laundry, or when she was going to upcycle bits of furniture homeless people wouldn't sleep in. One time, she decided she was going to buy and sell ornaments. Our whole living room looked like a graveyard for religious midgets thanks to all of the naked angels holding candles spread out around it.

Alas, no midgets had the chance to buy one. That business endeavour ended when my stepdad returned home early from a family BBQ and passed out on the bed. When my mum followed him a few hours later, safely armed with the new knowledge that he was cheating on her with a sister of a sister-in-law (note: that was inaccurate and happened years later! Don't worry about it) and raging because he'd taken too long to unlock the door for her, she smashed them all up in a show of strength and defiance.

She basically went full Greek, breaking one after the other until the living-room floor looked like a cat's litter box.

The police were called by one of the neighbours, and it all ended in both Mum and my stepdad getting a night's free stay at Her Majesty's finest hotel, also known as 'The Cells'.

Adam, however, got some free exercise prior to his stay. He got taken in doing yoga.

Limber Adam, as we like to call him, told the police officers they were not permitted access to our porcelain-carpeted house, and when they forced their way into the house saying they were on 'official police business', an altercation broke out that saw my stepdad finger the five-O's eyeball while briefly putting him in and then out of a headlock.

Adam recalls having no option other than to throw himself to the floor of our hallway in a bid to protect himself from the back-up officers that were flooding our usually far more inconspicuous, police-free house. The policeman had not enjoyed being cuddled tightly around the neck, nor being stroked gently on the eyeball, as it turned out, so the gaggle of officers gathered him into a pretzel and carted him off to Bell Street for a night in prison in nothing but his boxers.

Are any of you thinking what I'm thinking: I'm 100% getting arrested every time I'm in Dundee forever thanks to my memories of spewing and stand-up spooning police officers. I have not thought this through.

But back to the point in hand: I was teetering on the edge of psychosis and was fairly certain that the flies' air patterns were coded messages. At the time, Adam was away on his first offshore trip and Big Max was living less like she had sand in her crack and more like she had sunshine, so we were getting on better in general, as was she with the rest of the world. I pointed to the ceiling and said, 'What if those flies are actually writing important messages to us, but we have to flip it around because they aren't upside down?'

She howled with laughter that could be mistaken for a wounded hog and said, 'Only psychotics would think such a thing.' She continued to laugh at me until her eyes watered.

Little did she know I was going through a terrible mid-teen crisis in which I was unnaturally paranoid and thought I was the real-life *Truman Show* ... again. That's normal, right?

Am I a she-woman-devil? Is this book going to land me in an asylum? Do they do juice cleanses in there, and what about wine? Asking for myself.

Thankfully, I grew out of such a phase, and not only do I wish all flies death, I know that I'm

98.87982374% probably not psychotic or on *The Truman Show*.

Told her I'd thought about pushing her out of the kitchen window

There she was, just hanging out the window like easy prey. She looked like a piñata waiting to be hit with a bat. And, like the alert hunter to the sleeping fox, I was seeing an opportunity that might never present itself again.

I ran through the process in my head: take off in a sprint towards her, push her out the window and look down to make sure she wasn't hanging onto the clothes line; if she was hanging onto the clothes line, shake it violently, lock window immediately, discombobulate stepdad and run to Gran's house, just a short 14 miles away. Then it hit me, the fatal flaw, the pus-filled blemish, the weakness and the glitch: the off-chance she survived the four-storey fall from the kitchen window to the cold, hard ground waiting silently beneath.

I knew that if she did, not even a broken leg and missing foot would keep her down there long enough for me to escape the utter destruction she would dish out, aka the beating of a lifetime. Not to mention there was no way I'd make it all the way down the four flights of stairs to check if the building's back door was locked and all the way back up in time to push her out.

She was, at that point, hanging out the last sock from the basket, and soon the sun would dry the washing and I would be asked to take it in.

I let the chance slip by me.

Thirteen-year-old me was quite distraught about it for a short time. Thirty-year-old me wonders if any of this is even remotely normal. Am I a monster? Should I get help? What if my children are worse people than me? Maybe I should just sell my ovaries ... Different book for a different time.

When I finally came clean about my plan a few years later, she laughed hysterically and told me that there was, in fact, no chance the doctors had messed up at the hospital in '88 – I was undoubtedly her daughter. And then she asked in a far more serious tone if I'd had similar thoughts since, to which I replied that I hadn't. If I couldn't go through with it then, in such a perfect setting as the one the gods had given me that day, then my career as a parent-murderer was doomed and so already over.

She then proceeded to call our family and friends and let them know who the real monster in the family was.

My crown was taken from me because I was too truthful, and now it's in print. I am fucked. Amen.

Told her I'd said to my friend's mum that she'd told me said mum was a lesbian

My friend's mum was a lesbian. I didn't understand the stigma and/or stereotypes attached, and so when I went to said friend's house, I just came right out and asked her what it was like to be a bean-flicker.

It's not insensitive – that's what some people called lesbians back then. Men can be bean-flickers too, but they rarely know where it is.

It wasn't the informative answer I'd hoped for. That good old feisty lesbian answered my question with a keen one of her own: 'Who told you I was a lesbian?' she said, without even the slightest hint of fish-breath. (Another myth about that community. Also not insensitive. It's a joke. Everyone calm down.)

It was at that point I understood from the look in her beady, inquisitive eyes that I'd stepped into a metaphorical minefield and that the safest course of action was to lie.

A schoolmate had actually told me. She was carrying stories as children do. I felt that letting poor 'Lizzie' (as we will call her for the sake of not being sued) know that the whole of our school was privy to her romantic disposition was cruel, and so I lied and told her my mum had told me. That way she'd know an adult had told me and that there was nothing to worry about.

And that turned out not to be the case.

Big Max told me I'd better get over there the next day and confess, which I did not, but I did tell her that the confession had taken place and that Lizzie had forgiven and forgotten. PLOT TWIST: she later found out that was a lie.

Fast forward to 31 January 2015, when she attended what's known to many as the gay bar in Dundee, with her friend. She told me she'd been reintroduced to my schoolfriend's mum and that Lizzie had expressed her loathing for her in a myriad of ways, including expressive dance, hand gestures, eye hate, hair flipping, face twisting and the good old mouthing of the words 'fuck you', to name but a few.

I started out by offering the explanation that maybe Lizzie just hated her in general, or maybe she was wearing something offensive to lesbians, or maybe it was just her Resting Bitch Face syndrome haunting her again and making lesbians and straight people everywhere hate her. But seemingly there's no other way to take verbal confirmation of, 'You told your bairn I was a dyke, you arsehole.' This also served to seal my title as the family's worst liar.

For those of you who are not Scottish, translating that rancorous sentence spat by Lizzie at my mum, it turns into: 'You informed your guiltless daughter I was part of the lesbian community, you dreadful being.'

A personal note to Lizzie: I'm sorry, and it wasn't her.

PS. I heard your interpretive dance moves are second to none!

A note to the gay community: love is love. Let's not hate on me for repeating things that weren't insensitive in the early 2000s. Please. I'm sorry. Thank you. F*ck the Republicans, and praise be to Lady Gaga, Madonna and Bernie Sanders.

Got her clothes pegs for Christmas

She never let it go. She brings it up every Christmas. What she fails to mention is that six months before, for her birthday, I got her a 99p red nail polish. She also neglects to tell people that she hates gifts you can't use. ('They are such a waste of money.') Hence why this year I got her a new iron. She also neglects to tell of the hate-gifts I gave her yearly as a teen. Do you know how much energy is expended on annoying your parents? I – technically – gave her my youth.

Told her girls were mean to me

She told me to name them and tell me the names of their mothers. She remains confident she wasn't overbearing or overprotective.

Tried smoking

After this unfortunate incident, and I mean the part where I was caught, she made me smoke ten in a row and told me that if she ever smelled smoke on me again, I wouldn't receive so much as a rusty 1p piece from her.

All in all, it worked as well as cancer and I never took up the habit, so who says tough love doesn't work? I do, and here's why ...

Took advantage of a two-for-one offer

She once sent me to the store just behind our house in Americanmuir Road in Dundee, so I must have been about 11. I clambered through the green, leafy hedge at the back of the house, ran through the small field at the back of that and then propelled myself over the wall – the last obstacle between me and the snacks that could give a lesser person diabetes.

She had, in previous years, conditioned me to enjoy the trips to the store. She'd say that she was going to time me and we'd see if I could get my fastest time yet, and sometimes she'd throw in extra money for a bar of chocolate.

This particular time, she sent me for an onion, a pint of milk and a pack of Mr Kipling's French Fancies. It turned out that our luck was in and Mr Kipling was having a 'twofer', as we call it – meaning if you bought one pack of cakes, you could walk out with a second pack for nothing and you wouldn't be prosecuted for shoplifting.

After I'd gotten back after doing the maths and working out we had enough money for the free box of cakes, I placed them on the counter in the kitchen and stood to the side quietly to await my applause.

It never came.

A little maths challenge, if you will: if one onion and one pint of milk hit the back of your head and a woman who sounds like a man is chasing you, how long would it take you to get out?

The answer is FAF (fast as f*ck – a reliable unit of measurement). You move Usain Bolt fast.

Post-onion she screeched, 'You greedy little bastard! Why on God's green earth would we need two packs?'

I don't know, Max ... TO EAT PERHAPS!

I threw myself down the stairs towards our front door like I was getting chased by a slinky, clambered onto my faithful purple-and-black bike and, like a two-tyre Hot Wheels, peddled myself towards Auntie Jenny's house, where I stayed until Big Max summoned me home the following day ... After she'd eaten the damn French Fancies.

What she is able to calmly say now, here in the present day, is that she wouldn't have been able to enjoy only one or two of the delicious, dainty sponge fancies with delicious vanilla topping, drenched in soft fondant icing. No. She would, in fact, have had to have eaten them all. If only she'd said that, I'd have taken care of that second pack in no time at all. Straight down and on with their journey to the poop chute it would have been.

I will forever associate Mr Kipling's pastel-coloured cakes with abuse and perfect aim.

Guiding tip: When you're the beneficiary of a free second anything, eat/use before returning home.

The main
difference
between
adulthood and
childhood:
when you phone
someone
as a child, you're
hope they
pick up.

Cut myself bangs

I was small enough still to fit into my hiding spaces and wear my nighty all day without anyone saying a word, so let's assume I was about six when I cut myself bangs so short that you would've needed rice to curl them.

I was at my gran's and had been phoning her for days because she was about 12 late in picking me up. So, finally, I heard the door being knocked on and I heedlessly forgot about the cardinal sin I'd committed earlier in the stay as I ran to answer it the way we'd all run to a margarita truck now.

At first, she smiled at me like a one-man fan-band – obviously: we'd had a two-week break after she'd told my gran she'd be back 12 days earlier – but it quickly vanished for what was to be months.

She took one look at my already large forehead poking out from my barbed, prickled baby bangs and flew into a shouting fit so violent that I'm sure the deaf neighbour winced.

She made it seem as if I'd given myself a skinhead and used the scissors to scratch in a facial tattoo from the way she went on and on and on and on and on and on and on and on. My poor gran, in trying to defuse the situation, caught the shockwaves of Big Max's wrath-quake when she said, 'It's not that bad! Look, now you can see more of her face!'

Big Max flitted around and told her own mother, probably 25% of my genetic make-up, that seeing more of my face probably wasn't a good thing.

It sounds harsh, but she wasn't entirely wrong. I was missing two of my front teeth and so my top lip was collapsing in a bit, too.

Big Max recently accomplished a similar feat: there's a video online somewhere of her nearly crying because she used serrated-edge scissors to cut in her fringe.

Do you remember *Stars in Their Eyes*? It was essentially the best karaoke show ever, ever, ever made. The mist cleared, and the contestant emerged looking like their lyrical hero and then tried to sing like them, too.

So, what happened in an Airbnb in Marina del Rey, California, was that Big Max emerged from the mist of the shower looking like Friar Tuck, and I, the audience, creased while she tried to flatten the spikes against her now fully exposed forehead. Made my day, that did.

Guiding tip: Cut from underneath. Use a bowl as a template if necessary.

Ran away from her and then locked her out

Ah, this is essentially my crowning moment as a daughter. Behold poetry in action ...

'Watch your mouth, young lady!' followed by the infamous, 'Get back here, you little basket case!' were the words carried on the wind as I sprinted from my auntie's kiosk to her empty house. Big Max was fast, but she was never as fast as me. Thank you to the gods of medium-length legs.

After what was intended as a hysterical response to something very parentish that she'd said that didn't land as intended, I had no choice but to full-out sprint towards my auntie's house and, hopefully, safety.

When I say I was a good runner, I don't think it's an exaggeration to compare me to Forrest Gump in style, mental capacity and pace. I mean I was like a gloriously blonde (some would say ginger) whippet dancing through the air with long strides sturdily carrying me towards safety – in this example, at least.

I paced onwards fuelled by the fear of the foot that wished to make contact with my arsehole. I galloped three long streets and a driveway, flew through the dark wooden door, and sealed it off as though a swarm of short-horned grasshoppers were following me, which might have been preferable.

I also knew the secret entrance to the house and so proceeded to, and then climbed in through, the bathroom window; it was a foot wide and only Big Max and I were capable of going through it. I locked it up tight and thwarted that avenue of attack for her, too. She, under breath-arrest, stood in the stoned driveway, telling me I was dead when she finally got in.

Even after such an inspirational speech, I found myself terribly uncooperative. I sat on the kitchen bunker and had what I assumed was my last meal – a Taxi biscuit and a glass of cherryade – and I remember it to be nothing short of completely delightful.

She made her way to the kitchen window and, upon seeing my gleeful face indulging, became quite erratic.

'Get your arse down from there right now and open that door, you little shit!'

Again, this was not the call to action I would have chosen, and so I hopped down from the countertop and made my way to the dining room to make a private call.

I called my gran to calmly ask her advice while consuming my second Taxi biscuit, also glorious for each soon-to-be-rigor-mortised taste bud.

Before my wee old grandma, probably out trying to spot *antiques* in B&Q again, could pick up the phone, apparently ringing utterly devoid of the urgency on the other side, I heard Big Max's little feet pad furiously down the stairs behind me, two at a time no less.

My mouth began to dry and my eyes widened. She had her own secret way in she'd never told me about. I could hardly believe the audacity of her! How dare she not tell me of all of the secret entrances and exits in and out of my own aunt's house! I almost threw my third Taxi at her in protest and outrage, but it was just reaching melting point in my trouser pocket and would have been a futile defence strategy.

When she reached the last step of the stairs and burst through the door that they lay behind, there was a moment in which we were standing like Billy Hoyle and Sidney Deane, or Neo and Agent Smith.

Morpheus was clearly having a grand old time at a fete or chain-smoking on her veranda, because she was not picking up the goddamn, good-for-nothing phone.

In the end, she clouted me a force-ten hit round the head and dragged me by the arm, shoulder, butt and hair to the porch to think about my actions, where I did do exactly that. I thought about what I'd do differently and how much longer she'd have been forced to sit outside if I'd only known about that third way in the house (up the drainpipe and through the upstairs window).

I also thought about how different life at school would have been if I could've gone in the next day and regaled everyone with the tale of how I'd managed to keep her outside all night.

I was busy imagining how I'd have been the proof that not all heroes wear capes and spandex when I remembered the chocolate biscuit in my pocket, which was now more akin to a small smoothie. I licked my way through my third Taxi, laughing at the thought of Big Max's short, stout, near useless legs and waiting on someone to retrieve me from the locked porch.

Guiding tip: Always have snacks handy.

Asked her if the lights went off when I blinked

We were walking through Asda when I discovered the energy that is light. I was opening and closing my eyes in an effort to see whether or not I was Jesus, and if I could beat the lights and open my eyes before they came back on.

After several failed attempts, I started to question my theory. I turned to my mum for the answer, which was my first mistake.

'Mum, do the lights go off and on when I blink?'

'What do you think, Max?' (Said like kind of a salty b*tch.)

'Well, I don't know because my eyes are closed, and it might not work if I only close one eye.'

'It only works if you do it and don't talk.'

What a cun-itch. That's right, I said it. I called her both c*nt and b*tch in the same sentence and no, I'm not that proud of it. And yet the sentence has survived multiple proofreading rounds and request for removal. Let's just think about this... If she hadn't lied to me, I might have become a scientist. A white, but stupid, Neil deGrasse Tyson. Terrible parenting, Big Max, terrible! You might have single-handedly ruined humanity and forfeited me my place in Science Heaven, AKA The Nobel Peace Prize Hall of Fame.

It wasn't too long after that incident that I asked her when a shot glass got big enough to be called a bucket. Saltily, she replied it was when it held enough gin to make questions seem fun. She's quick when her replies are intended to hurt.

Took too long to pick sweets

If you really wanted to be on her shit-list, you could do any of the following:
- Not fluff her cushions after you'd sat near them
- Walk on the rug in the middle of the room
- Lose any item of clothing
- Leave crockery in your room
- Be under eight years old and four feet tall and take too long to pick a sweetie

Once a week I was allowed a treat, which, looking back, is fair enough given that I was probably pre-diabetic by the end of each weekend with my gran.

Every Sunday, on our way home, we'd go in Simara's in Ardler and she would tell me I could pick one sweetie.

I always stood still and quiet, surveying the shelves like I was looking for signs of life. I was mentally going through the tastes of each sweet and what qualities they had to offer me and my finely adapted taste buds.

It was almost like meditation, except I never, ever, *ever* got to reach enlightenment. She used to stand like a tanned Grinch at the back of me, counting down and saying things like, 'If you don't pick a sweetie within the next ten seconds, you won't get one at all.'

Sometimes, sugary dreams don't come true. Although I have no idea what she was trying to teach me. Working under pressure? Time management? Either way, it sucked, and it probably laid the foundation of my binge eating in adulthood.

Some might say Big Max owes me multiple rounds of lipo – and by 'some' I mean one, and by 'one' I mean me, and by 'me' I mean 'I'm fucked because she's poor.'

Guiding tip: Cancel out binge eating with salads on Mondays and then wine as a replacement meal Tuesdays, Wednesdays and Thursdays.

Nearly re-entered the room after my bird died

We had just moved from the tenement in Ardler – the house where I was hit on the head with a hammer – to a flat in the Pentland area, where there were no children to bully or befriend me.

The flat was colder than winter in Westeros and we both hated it. We had our own furniture plus the woman's furniture whose house it was. We had to climb over her sofa, table and fridge to get to bed, which I kind of liked because every day I'd pinball off the mattress that stood against the wall onto our own and pivot onto my side just in time to watch her hit her knee off of the *spare* dressing table we'd inherited.

And when we weren't in the mood for trying to catch hypothermia or one another's company, we'd go to my gran's and make her day a misery. I'm sure she loved it.

Pre Scruffy, the Scooby Doo of porn, I'd begged for a dog for *forever*, but the all-powerful Big Max was scared of little dogs, and so I had to settle for a canary and a goldfish.

The goldfish quickly died from overeating, the fat little bastard. (*Look, there aren't measuring devices for goldfish food and I, as a nine-year-old, found the goldfish to look hungry … even when he was bloated, which is why Oxfam adverts should be banned, because it's just confusing. You're welcome. I know, there should be more people like me in the world to do the thinking for all of us.*)

The canary – named, in a show of complete originality, Tweety Pie – survived longer, although not much longer.

We'd started spending more and more time at my gran's house, but poor Tweety didn't get the invite for a while. He was left too long on his own before we brought him with us, and so either he got really excited, because my gran's house was warm and she let him out the cage a lot, and, in his twittery excitement, had a heart attack, or he was so dismayed at the time he was now spending with us that he was forced to throw himself from his perch onto the cold, hard metal floor of the cage in a successful suicide attempt.

I also think the latter.

I had just left my gran's living room when I heard a feathery thud and turned to head back in. My mum splayed herself over the door, blocking it like she was the stone to Jesus's tomb.

'Mum, let me in. It's me!'

'Don't know any "me"s here. Go to bed!'

And so I did. I stamped all the way down the hall, because what child in the Western world does what they are told politely?

She told me the next morning that T. P. was no longer with us and offered me a shoebox and a spoon to dig him a shallow grave. I looked around at the cage to see that poor T. P. was splayed out at the bottom looking more like a feathered starfish than a bird scared of cats.

Thankfully, he was yellow, so the colour of death didn't do much to his complexion, and I buried him and made a little gravestone out of a sheet of A4 laminated in Sellotape. I still was not granted permission for a dog.

Guiding tip: Have an adult you trust look at the situation and advise the best course of tactical manipulation in order to gain a pet when your parent helped kill your last one. Do the same for other children when you get older.

Told her my aunt and uncle used me as a drug mule

I was heavily into music when I was younger – all types, from Celine Dion to the Charlatans and Oasis. My aunt and uncle were heavily into music and dope – all kinds of dope, from hash to weed – and being all hippie-like and free, they took me to a lot of music festivals with them. All of which felt like the musical cocoons that would one day release my inner girl-band butterfly.

Anyway, when they took me to festivals with them, they would always make me carry the backpack. It was a glorious rucksack that fitted all the things one young girl could ever need in it: a lot of drugs and alcohol, a bottle of water, and a snack.

'Right, hen,' my uncle would say, 'on you go. Don't look worried now!'

And I didn't.

Drug-muling is pretty easy. Basically, you're like a flat-land hiker. You just walk around with a backpack on and smile at adults.

I did, however, make the mistake of telling my mum that I was a part-time drug mule and that I was thinking of getting into it when it was work experience time at school.

She said no and she needed answers.

It seemed a lot like she was holding back on having a heart attack and partial stroke. She didn't beat me or my aunt and uncle to the point that we all looked as though we had been born with birth defects, but that was only because she recalled that one time she herself had used me as a mule for my dad (Gary/Jesus) when he'd 'acquired' and stuffed my diaper with phone-box money.

I think he *allegedly* broke into the part of the phone box where the cash is stored, *allegedly* gathered the monies and definitely sprinted home like Linford Christie had possessed him. Then I was weighed down with 20p pieces and the prayers of my two parents not to take a shit lest the police come and ask about our silver store.

Guiding tip: Get yourself a family that can do both.

Failed to be grateful enough

This was roughly around the time I hated her more than I'd ever hated her previously combined.

We were going through a little patch in which she thought I was ungrateful and I thought life would be great if she skedaddled to literally anywhere else in the world and we never saw one another ever, ever again.

I was allowed into two rooms of our five-room house: the bathroom and my own bedroom. She'd summoned me from my hate den to the kitchen door to collect my dinner, at which point – or so I hoped – I'd slip quietly back into my room and we could both get on with pretending the other didn't exist for the following 12 hours. It would've worked out fine, but she ruined it because the one thing she loves more than silent loathing is a fight.

Has anyone else pondered the age-old conundrum of how parents can always hear you say 'I hate you' under your breath, but never a quiet 'thanks'? If so, keep reading, because you'll find another example here, but not a solution. None exist.

I stomped up to the kitchen door, really threw the arch in my back so she could tell with a glance that I was standing like I hated her and waited for her to hand me a plate of food that a starving African village would chuck. She handed me the plate and I talked at a normal teenage level and mumbled thank you. The next thing I was aware of was my pulse throbbing against the sharp edge of a knife.

This is it, I thought to myself. Her face was so close to my head that it was like she was trying to blow-dry my hair with her breath. I did exactly what Planet Earth tells you not to do, ever, in any circumstance ... I ran for it. Think lion. Think gazelle. Think death. Specifically, the nearing of mines.

I did not get far.

She says – and we don't believe her – that in the heat of the moment, she did not notice (nor care) that the butter knife was at my throat, held steadfast by her unquivering and ultra-masculine arm.

You could be forgiven for presuming that was not her first time nearly knifing someone in the neck, but I guess we'll never know. It wasn't until she snatched the plate from my dead-still grip and threw it at the wall that the knife was taken from its resting place by my jugular. I honestly thought she was going to turn my head into a kebab over some unthanked potatoes!

I made my second attempt to run for it and succeeded. Unskewered, unloved and underfed.

Part Six: Things She's Made Up

That she'd bought me a car

I was desperate to drive from a very early age in life. There was nothing more appealing to me than the thought of getting into a car and driving really far, really fast.

For the first 16 years, I had to make do with a bicycle with a lollipop stick wedged between the brake and the tyre, and my imagination, but there was just something so alluring about the thought of having a car and the freedoms I thought came with one (obviously I didn't know about MOTs or tax). No one knew how I felt better than Big Max.

One day, I walked into my kitchen and saw a can of window defroster sitting on the table. I looked from my mum to my stepdad, trying to curb my excitement in case it was all just one cruel joke. My mum clicked on straight away and my stepdad followed suit.

'Do you think we got you a car?' she asked me warmly through a smile.

I nodded gently, while battling with my eyebrows for dominance because they were trying to do a celebratory Mexican wave.

'And if you had to guess, what car would you say we picked for you?'

At that point in my life, I was finding it hard to decide between two cars: I either wanted a 1995 Renault Clio or a 2002 Ferrari F40 (both pictured below).

'Ummm, a Fer ... Clio?'

'Well, look, we couldn't afford a Ferrari, obviously, but we did manage a Clio! Come look out the window,' she said sweetly, guiding me from the table over to the kitchen window.

We stood looking and I couldn't see a Clio anywhere. I was starting to panic; what if they'd bought me the wrong car? Should I pretend that it was a Clio and they'd got it right so I didn't seem ungrateful, or should I let them know that the defroster was going to be used on something a lot less savoury than a Renault?

I didn't have to say a thing. They – my life examples – erupted into howling laughter and left me standing in the kitchen with two eyebrows that were now being dragged down with the weight of the tears falling from their counterparts. There was no sign of an eyebrow Mexican wave for a fortnight.

They did, however – once the laughter had ceased and my mum had managed to claw her way out of laughing-foetal on the kitchen floor – tell me they would buy me a car when I was 17 and could drive, but they hadn't that particular day because they thought I should learn in an instructor's car. What's that, you say? You smell heaps of bullshit? Yeah, I must have had a blocked nose that day, because I believed.

I know what you're thinking: *Let it go! Grow up. Move on. Oh, Max, she was just having some fun!*
Absolutely not. She's a repeat offender.

Let me take you back to '92, to the fourth birthday of a child born into a special kind of hell. I woke up early and snuck into the living room. The only thing I'd heard about for weeks was my birthday.

People were always asking me what I wanted, how old I was going to be, what kind of cake I liked. I was pretty excited!

I turned on the big light and looked around. There weren't any banners or decorations like there had been at my nursery friend's house, nor were there any gifts wrapped or cards or really anything to indicate it was 29 October and my fourth birthday. I did what I had to do. I summoned the beast at 5 a.m.

When she came around, she politely informed me it was too early to be my birthday and we were to sleep until 10 a.m.

Not too long after that, my auntie Joe came and the party finally got started. Big Max sat me on the sofa and handed me my only gift: a bag of penny sweets. Her face looked more disappointed than mine when I took them and said thanks.

She was like, 'Ummmm, didn't you want anything else? It's your birthday, remember?'

'Can I watch cartoons?'

She was really starting to look perplexed. 'Yeah, but you know that's all you got for your birthday, right?' I nodded and looked to the TV, only a little bit sad there was no cake or yo-yos.

Finally, after Rosie and Jim concluded another dramatic show, she went back to using me like a really short human slave; she sent me to get her something from the cupboard at the bottom of the hallway, and, upon opening it, I started squealing as if I'd found the portal to Narnia.

'Mummy! Mummy! Look!' I yelled at her, holding my crotch in case I peed myself.

There in the cupboard I'd been sent to, in order to fetch her something probably made up, was a bike and a shit-ton of other presents. I squealed my way up and down the hallway of our house on my new bike until my legs gave out.

The same could not be said about the car she promised me. Again, I got zero cars. Zero surprises and one can of defroster. Which is another reason why I could never work out why my stepdad was so infuriated when I stole – nay, *borrowed* – his car one night as he slept.

I mean, it *could've* been because I backed the red, very unresponsive Ford into a lamppost that wasn't there when I checked my mirror only moments before, used all of his petrol and then tried to pretend I didn't even know where he kept his keys the next morning. We'll never know.

Alas, his wasn't the only car I *borrowed*, so to speak. Both prior to that and afterwards, I borrowed my aunt Linn's car, and when she was sharp enough to keep a note of the miles SHE was driving and then ask me about the extra miles I was driving as she slept, I told her it must have been that she was parking it on a hill and that the car must've been moving a little bit each night, resulting in 267 extra miles on the meter in a week.

Something in my story was intensely flawed, and she said she didn't believe me, so I shouted at her and called her a monster for catching me.

Was there a pattern developing? I don't know.

My other aunt – introduced to you earlier as Louise, who was really a good egg – let me borrow her car, but when she gave me petrol money to fill it up, I'd give it to my then boyfriend, 'Bert', and he'd steal the petrol knowing that the cameras at Tesco's garage on Harefield Road weren't good enough to pick up the licence plate, and we'd live like kings on pizza from the luxurious establishment known to thousands as Domino's.

I also borrowed my room-mate's car, which she had for learning in. I kept a spare traffic cone in my room so that I could temporarily exchange it with the car. That way, I always knew that when I returned home, I would get that specific space back. This would result in her being none the wiser when she returned home from work each night, or so I thought.

When she found out, she made it seem as though I'd crashed the car into her family home, wiped out her entire family and then taken a sh*t on her mum's bed.

All of this could have been avoided if my mum and stepdad had just bought me a banger. But no, they've caused harm to many people and families all over Dundee.

Source: cardomain.com

Butter on my slippers

She had me believing (for two or three texts) that this was a real, widely used saying, but it turns out it's about as common as Fritzl's friends. She used it in place of 'I'd be out of there like a whippet'. But this is mild in comparison to some of the other things that woman has told me.

Your dad is ...
i. dead
ii. in the military
iii. dead to us

Even after these three, she still maintains that every kid should know who their father is, 'Hence,' she'll say, 'why yours is on your birth certificate.' But she doesn't mind if you think your dad is dead.

Ah, cognitive dissonance, how you shape a fine world.

We were walking from our second house in Lindrick Court, so I must have been about three or so, and she'd not long gotten me back with some suspicious burns on both of my legs and a hateful attitude towards her, which might have been there before, but who knows.

My father had taken me one weekend, against his will, and in retaliation had kept me for a couple of months after.

No one thinks my own dad burned my legs. The theory was that his girlfriend at the time didn't like me very much and I was perhaps – ahem – 'warmly' mistreated.

My dad would've had no idea, because I was in my pyjamas by the time he came home every night and he didn't dress me in the mornings.

I don't really remember any of it, so no damage done – unless they are super-rich now, in which case I live on the brink of a fiery breakdown each and every waking moment.

Anyway, after the whole charade was over and my mum had stolen me back after grooming a little girl to help her (not quite as creepy as I've just made it sound), I asked for my dad, and my mum told me he was dead and that he'd been hit by a 'very large truck'. She maintains to this day that I wasn't upset about the tragic news I'd been half orphaned, but you can never tell with her.

After a while, she proceeded to tell me the truth. She said, 'Okay, I have something to tell you. Are you listening?'

'Yes, Mum,' I replied diligently, hoping she was about to tell me something glorious like maybe we were going on a trip, but separately.

She said to me, 'Do you remember when I told you your dad was dead?'

I nodded, signalling I did indeed.

'Well, I didn't tell the truth.' She paused, trying to find the right words. 'He didn't get run over at all.'

'So, no big truck hit him, and I don't have to wear matching underwear every day in case one hits me?' I asked, ending with a truck noise followed by something meant to sound like a splat.

'You do have to wear matching pants and vest every day, Max, because you aren't a barbarian, but no, Gary, your dad, he wasn't hit by a truck. He was killed in the war.'

'What war?'

'There's a war, but it happens when little children sleep.'

The End. Until ...

My aunt Joe caught wind of the tale, thanks to me telling all the adults and children who would listen that there was a silent war raging on and my dad was killed in it. Eventually, it all came out. Gary was dead. But only dead to us.

Thankfully, Gary wasn't able to say the same about us, and he was forced to give me £3.57 every two weeks in order to help my mum support me.

Thanks, Gazza, I've been saving and soon I'll have enough for absolutely nothing useful in my adult life.

However, if it wasn't for the Red Witch of Dundee, I probably would've spent some time with him. But not knowing him for this long has let me hold on to the hope that I'm not just my mother's daughter.

My sister

She had me believing that I had a sister for at least two or three years of my life.

The trouble with Maddison, other than the fact she was fake and it took me three years to realise it, was that she was always better at everything than I was. She supposedly always tidied her room, went to bed when she was told, washed in the bath, ate her veggies and just really showed me up the whole time.

I can't remember how it came about that she'd made her up, but I distinctly remember she didn't seem sorry about the three-year lie. Sad.

Her middle name

I found out at the young age of 22 that she'd also been lying to me about having a middle name. Mine, however, isn't fake. No, she actually gave me the middle name Irene.

Hers, though, that's more fictitious than unicorn shit. She told me very nonchalantly as I filled out her ESTA application that she has no middle name and had just given herself one because she liked the name Marie.

That I just turned my pants inside out

Some of you might think I started this one. And you'd be right. My mum had always told me that if

I ever saw someone stealing (especially from us), I should always tell. So, basically, she was willingly raising a snitch. Anyway, I did see someone stealing: her.

Okay, so I don't *really* know what I saw, which is just as good as seeing someone steal, and so that's what I told everyone. An executive decision was made, and the witness account was taken by the whole family.

I told them all my mum had gone into my aunt Deb's bag and so she was definitely stealing and we should all hide the purses my pocket money came from. Obviously, my aunties explained that Big Max wasn't stealing and it was sometimes okay to go into someone's bag if you knew them – usually if they asked you to.

Some parents would let it slide. Maybe just make the child apologise or, even better, explain to the child the implications of saying something like that. But not my parent! She told my whole family that I had worn the same pants for four days in a row and that she wasn't sure, but, quite plausibly, I may have also turned them inside out on day three. And so that's how I came to be known as Pissy Pants.

I tasted my own medicine, and it was bitter. Bitter!

My (insert family member here) died (I'll always keep you alive)

I have currently been employed by around 68 fine establishments and have been paid by most of them fairly for a wide range of services, including serving quality alcoholic beverages to middle-aged men on Monday mornings, cleaning an airplane-parts factory and stealing the boss's Marks and Spencer biscuits. I've also worked in nurseries, even though I find children repulsive and selfish, as well as working as a cold-call seller, a berry picker, a leaflet handler, a sales assistant, a pancake maker, an optician's assistant, a shelf-stacker, a call-centre person for Tesco's supermarket, an ROV pilot and technician, a hacker, a digital forensics 'expert' … and the busy list goes on.

My mum? League. Of. Her. Own.

She's had more jobs than the red-light district. She's probably had more jobs than all of Jamaica combined, and she's never been sacked in her life, mainly because someone in the family always dies.

The death pattern: she calls the employer – which is really the only thing the house phone was allowed to be used for – and it all starts with an emergency in the family, usually her dad. If she feels she wants to go back after a couple of days, he doesn't die. If she wants a new job, then he dies and she just never goes back, and it's because she's finding it 'very difficult to handle'.

Sometimes, she does go back after a short week/week and a half off and then, soon after that, shockingly, and in a severe and heinous downturn in her made-up life, her stepmum dies, too. Even though she doesn't have a stepmum. But that's just about the full loop of the death pattern. Other people sometimes die, too. But never me. Amen.

She's always said to me, 'I'll always keep you alive and I'll never put you into a coma!' A mother's love really is the purest.

Guiding tip: To avoid verbally killing off your whole family to get out of work, have "*an accident at work that isn't your fault.*" #injurylawyersforyou

Thanks for coming to my TED Talk. Motivational speaking is a gift of mine.

(I'm sorry I wrote it.)

Things I did that might have made her this way

It's said that the quickest way to get your child's attention is to sit down and look comfortable. I'm inclined to believe that. However, the quickest way for a child to get their parent's attention is, undisputedly, to cease being noisy. For instance, I was caught ripping my Care Bear wallpaper off in pure silence one day because I thought that would better help my case in getting racing-car wallpaper. It didn't, in case you were holding on to a glimmer of hope just then.

For how childlike I am as an adult, I was sort of smart for a child: I once managed to open the child-resistant lock on my gran's child-friendly morphine. That's sadly and quite inconveniently – for me – where the smartness ends. I had to get rushed to hospital and my stomach pumped to free me from the evil, yet very relaxing, clutches of morphine. I also ate her cigarettes once, too. I was pretty certain that that was what all the adults were doing, and so I had tobacco-scented dumps for about a week after. I obviously misread the situation.

I also chose to die one day when my bike's brakes failed on the Timex Brae. It was that or scuff my new white trainers, but given she'd already told me she'd kill me if I scuffed my new white trainers, I opted for death by speed.

The brakes failed mid-hill, and as my mum ran after me, and a very busy road stood before me at the bottom of the hill, my life flashed before my eyes. I was like, *Holy shit snacks! I'm really glad about all of the good things that have happened to me in this short 13 years of my life, like petting all those dogs and getting my friends to let me be Sporty Spice and not Ginger, but I am boiling at her for stealing my pocket money, that gypsy devil woman!*

The end

This book might seem to some people like a detailing of a single parent's pitfalls and stumbles, but I hope that to everyone else, it will be exactly that, but also hilarious.

But really, in all seriousness, and as a final farewell: there is no love like a mother's love. There is never going to be someone who is truly your best friend the way your mother is. It's handed down in the very fabric of life and how life is made. But (tip:) to survive a mother's love, you have to remember that life doesn't come with a manual, it comes with a mum ... and who reads manuals anyway? While they are sometimes our last resort, we are their first thought.

A Guide is coloured to produce laughter from you and embarrassment from her. It's a short walk down a long lane of memories, and, of course, it's going to be judged and redefined by its readers, but it is what it is to those who read it, and to me it's a display of old ideas and parenting principles trying to govern the ever-changing trends of new generations.

It's also a presentation of what we all face as children and parents: instincts eluding the grasp of logic.

Just in case you've been able to see through the thin veneer of comedy I've coloured this dreadful book of heinous memories in, feel free to email her (abuse only please) at **bigmax@terriblemother.com**. It'll work out for us all, because I expect some of them will spawn a whole new book …

Welcome to the family, you made it!

Made in the USA
Monee, IL
19 January 2020

20523885R00154